THE STORY OF ONE WOMAN

A TESTIMONY

Dedication

I dedicate this book to
my Father in heaven who sent His son just for me.
To His son Jesus for coming and becoming
my Savior,
my King, and the lover of my soul.
To the Holy Spirit who guides me in all truth,
revealing the mysteries of heaven.
To all those who through prayer, friendship, parenting
and much correction, have helped me get this far.
May God continue to bring such people in my pat, as
my life unfolds.

Contents

Foreword

I was born again, as they say in the Christian church, on July 24, 1983. That makes me a mere 26 years old at the time this was written. Yes, I look a lot older than that, that is true. In the earth I am older but as a new creature in Christ I am only 26. That day I entered the Glory of God and began a different life. All things before then are but mere memories. They do not exist in the Kingdom. None of what happened to me before my re-birth is remembered by my Father God and never will be found in heaven. Only the things that I do, and have done after that day, are relevant. Never the less, I will recant some of those previous events for you. Not to give praise to the darkness but to give glory to the light of God.

Some may say this is pure imagination. There are two possibilities to this story. One, it is fictional in which case it will entertain you. The other, that it is true and will enlighten you.

Either way you decide which you choose to believe. May it only bring Honor to my Father in Heaven

1

In The Beginning

I was born in the U.S. to parents of from two different cultures. At the age of four we moved to the Caribbean and lived with my maternal grandmother for a season. Growing up my life was surrounded in spiritualism, witchcraft, divination and so on. Living in this environment it is easy to fall into this way of life. For most people it is a mixture of Catholicism and paganism. It was common in my family to have everyone over on Saturday nights and bring out the Ouija board. The men would play dominoes and the women would engage in necromancy *(the speaking and communicating with the dead).* I remember an instance when the table that the Ouija board was on came up off the floor and chased my uncle down the hall. The spirit controlling it was not happy, for he had been made fun of. This was all a part of life there.

At the age of 4 or 5 I was molested by the man who tended my grandmother's garden. That is when *a spirit of unworthiness* entered me. As he placed me on his lap, and molested me, he kept telling me that I was dirty and no good. No longer a happy little girl, I carried in my soul a hurt that would change and shape my life. I would sit alone and pray I was a nun like those who taught me at school.

Matthew 18:6
But if anyone causes one of these little ones who be-
lieve in me to sin, it would be better for him to have a
large millstone hung around his neck and to be
drowned in the depths of the sea.

As I matured, I grew in body and in the gifts God bestowed on me. I could see spirits clearly with my physical eyes. The first time this happened, I was 14 years old. I got up one night to get a drink of water. I passed the bedroom window and looked outside. There, in the dark of night, was a black figure, in the shape of a woman. She was in a flowing black dress. There she was, floating in the air, few feet off the ground, looking back at me. She startled me, but she did not vanish as you would think. She continued hovering as I looked on. It seemed to go on for the longest time. I remember that I was not moved by what I was seeing with my eyes. I decided to go back to bed and ignored her. I have never feared the spirit realm. Later that week I found out the mother of a friend had put a curse on me. Of course, that was remedied in the usual way by going to our spiritist and reversing what was done. Slowly, the devil began to take a hold of my life and was planning to use my gifts for his purposes.

Visiting a spiritist was, and is, a common thing in Latin countries. Any time there was a problem, that was what you did. You gathered the necessary herbs and oils and, proceeded to do what they required; all as offerings to a saint or a virgin (one of the many apparitions of the virgin Mary). The results were always as you wanted, but never lasted long. The spirit wanted more, so more problems would arise. It was a vicious cycle. So the spirit of witchcraft entered my life.

Leviticus 19:31
" 'Do not turn to mediums or seek out spiritists, for you will be defiled by them. I am the LORD your God.

We moved a lot while growing up due to my father's alcoholism. That was the way of dealing with it. I remember he would say, "If we move then I won't drink." Of course that did not work. It was very hard for me while growing up. Moving so often kept me from having any real friendships. School was always a struggle. In Puerto Rico I attended catholic school. In the United States I went to public school. It was difficult to go from a Spanish education to an English one. I was always the new kid and therefore the outsider, never to be let in. Picked on and abused verbally, I went through those years lonely and empty of any real companionship or relationships. I learned to let people use me so I could get their approval, and therefore, also learned to use other people. And so entered *a spirit of rejection.*

Psalm 94:14
For the LORD will not reject his people; he will never forsake his inheritance.

At home things were no better and weekends were always stressed. Friday's were always tense filled with worries of whether or not my father would make it home. I knew he would be drunk, and that there would be fighting between he and my mom. All I wanted was for him to get home safe. I would sit by the window for hours just waiting and praying to the many saints and virgins I had grown to know. I would offer them all I had so that they in turn, would grant my petition. Hours would go by, and with them suffering and pain in my stomach. Sooner or later he would arrive. I would go to bed knowing that even though he was home, it was not over. Then would come the morning. After hours of arguments, apologies would be spoken and promises given. All would fall to the ground by the next week. This was the way it was and I saw no other way. And so entered *the spirit of fear*

Psalm 27:1
The LORD is my light and my salvation— whom shall I fear? The LORD is the stronghold of my life— of whom shall I be afraid?

When I was 17 my father joined AA and stopped drinking and although that was a good thing, the many years of suffering had taken a toll on me. Being behind two years in high school made me the dummy, and no one would even give me the time of day. Alone and depressed were all my days that should have been joyful. At 17, I became engaged to marry a man 9 years my senior. I was looking for an answer. I was looking for peace and love. I believed this would be it. I would finally have an escape. Unfortunately, this was only another trap, and I fell in it. My fiancee did not believe I was a virgin and raped me. There I was. I had put myself in a position of no return. I trusted and believed in what I thought was love. Betrayed, used, and broken, I decided to end the engagement. I gave no explanations to anyone only to say it was not going to work. Deep in my heart, I was dying. I felt alone and had no hope. A few nights had passed and my mother was awakened by a spirit (demon). He told her that I had participated in sex. She came into my room in the middle of the night, outraged, she confronted me. She accused me of being promiscuous and piled a heap of guilt on me. She even implied that this could cause my father to start drinking again. Once more, there was disappointment on top of the pain and guilt I already felt. She said, "What will the neighbors think? What about the family? What if you are pregnant? You have to marry him!". And so entered *the spirit of guilt.*

Psalm 38:4
My guilt has overwhelmed me like a burden too heavy to bear.

Guilt now had a home in me. There I was trapped with no way out. I made the phone call to the very one I had run from. He came and agreed to do the right thing and marry me as my parents had demanded. I had lost everything. My trust and my dignity. Even the little bit of hope I had left was gone. Rumors of my so-called promiscuity spread through the school making it even harder to attend. I would walk the halls of the high school and could hear the laughter and the comments being said. I couldn't ride the bus and so I would walk four miles to and from in the heat of the day as others would drive by. I dropped out in my junior year and never returned. A few months later I married the man who took the last piece of my life. I figured it could not be any worse. I was wrong.

Pregnancy came 6 months later. I thought a baby would change things. Wrong again. He began to abuse me mentally. I endured ridicule and was treated as a servant. I would constantly be humiliated in front of his friends and family. When it finally escalated to physical abuse, I was done. I fell to the ground one day, propelled by the force of his push. Here I was 3 months pregnant and on the floor. Suddenly, coldness came over me. It was as if all that was within me, all that was left, suddenly died. I was empty of all emotions. I got up from the floor where I had landed and called my parents to come and get me. I was gone the next day. We separated then. I could not continue with the abuse and the lack of concern I was experiencing. Trapped between two bad places, I chose the lesser. Then *the spirit of abuse entered.* The divorce would not be final until after the baby was born. I found myself back in the house I wanted so much to leave. The drinking had stopped but the constant arguing and fighting for control had not. They both were now saved but I saw no difference in their lives. There was no peace. There had to be more. Somewhere, somehow there had to be more.

Hebrews 10:22
Let us draw near to God with a sincere heart in full assurance of faith, having our hearts sprinkled to cleanse us from a guilty conscience and having our bodies washed with pure water.

The Void

Deep in the soul of man,
There is an empty place.
Deep in the soul of man there is a hunger.
Deep in the soul of men there is a searching.

What is it thats lacking?
What is it that is so hidden?
Why is there a void
With such desire to fill?

So that man can go searching.
So that man can find.
So that man can fill this place,
With the only thing.

The only thing that satisfies.
The only thing that can fulfill all things.
The only thing that actually fit,
Perfectly in that space in the heart.

What is that thing?
It is the One, who created all that ever was.
The One who created all that ever is.
Who created all that ever will be.

It is God.

2

Dark ages

As time went on, and my life just moved on day by day, I reached for something to fill my soul. I began to practice spiritism, the religion so familiar to me. That practice of faith in saints and apparitions of virgins that I grew up with. I began to study the art of divination with tarot, psychometry, and witchcraft. It was easily achieved for me. I was good at it and enjoyed the fact that I was now getting attention. I believed that this would give me control of my life. I could finally get what I wanted and no one could get in the way. All I had to do was work the craft. Here now, in my life, entered control and manipulation which make up the *spirit of witchcraft.*

Deuteronomy 18:10-12
Let no one be found among you who sacrifices his son or daughter in the fire, who practices divination or sorcery, interprets omens, engages in witchcraft, or casts spells, or who is a medium or spiritist or who consults the dead. Anyone who does these things is detestable to the LORD,

I recall one day I was doing a favor for a friend by directing someone I didn't know through the city of Miami. I was sitting in the back seat 6 months pregnant, she kept looking at me through the rear view mirror. I was becoming very uncomfortable. Then suddenly she said, "You will have a boy and will meet your new husband soon after the birth". She was a spiritist. I looked at her and laughed. I had determined I was not going to remarry and I certainly didn't want a boy. It would be the one thing my ex wanted. She continued to talk and described the man I would marry. Older, gray hair, and Jewish. He would worship the ground I walked on. She told me I had many powers and was very gifted in the realm of the spirit. The day ended and I decided to ignore all she had said. My son, yes a son, was born a few months later to my surprise and the surprise of the doctor who had said it was definitely a girl.

It was a warm summer day four months after the birth. I was twenty. My neighbor invited me over to a small gathering. She also had a new baby boy and wanted all to come see him. I remember what I was wearing to this day, white bell-bottom pants, white halter top, a red beaded necklace and red platform shoes. It is funny how styles all come back around. There I was entering into her house. Suddenly, I looked up and there he was. All the hair on my arm stood on end. I knew it was him. I didn't have to talk, I knew. There he stood grey hair and Jewish. I became determined it would not be as the woman had said. I had no intention of going in that direction. Ha! I quickly moved into the kitchen to remove myself from his glaring looks. He followed me there only to find no conversation or even an acknowledgment of his existence. Few hours passed before I left to go home. I could no longer sit with his eyes on me. Victory! I got away.

Two weeks later, my neighbor called to ask if she could give this man my phone number. He was driving her crazy calling for it. I remember thinking, "Boy he is persistent." She begged and pleaded and I gave in. I gave her permission to pass the information requested. I figured, why not? I'll get a night out, a good meal, a movie and just make it the worst date he ever had. I figured that will end his pursuit. The date was in all standards a total flop. I was the most unsocial, rude person on the planet. Three weeks later, he was still on the hunt. Even though I tried to reject him, he just kept coming back. I did everything to discourage him. He was relentless. During this time, I had decided to enter nursing school and had begun my classes. On one of our dates, I read the tarot cards for him. "This may just push him away". I thought. In the reading I informed him that a friend of his would suddenly die. Within a two-day span he called me in total terror and forbade me to ever read the tarot for him again. He had just gotten a phone call. His friend was dead! It scared him. I was not surprised. It was what I was hoping for. My predictions had always been very accurate. This still did not deter him. What I had neglected to tell him in his reading was that he also would soon be married to a high priestess, me. I gave up and we got engaged. I finished nursing school and I converted to Judaism. We married a year after we met and shortly thereafter I had another son.

Proverbs 25:15
Through patience a ruler can be persuaded, and a gentle tongue can break a bone.

As time went on I became deeper involved in new age, meditation astrology, numerology, stones, and color therapies. I also researched American Indian magic. There is no area of new age and or of spiritism practices that I did not get involved in. For a short time I practiced Caribbean Santeria where I engaged in animal sacrifices to the saints (so they call them but in reality are demons). Blood was spilled for the favor requested of a saint. Promises and vows were given. The more you practiced the deeper and more involved I became. I recall the day I had enough of my ex- husband's aggravations. He was not re-married and was constantly causing me grief. I went to numerous spiritist and voodooists seeking for help. I did not want to harm him; I just wanted him to go away. I pursued this until the day came when one of these people asked me to offer my son to a particular god. She said that way he would always be covered by this saint. She gave me all the instructions for preparation and the date the service would be pre-formed. I went home and the more I thought about it, the more my spirit grew fearful. I decided that it was one thing for me to make a decision like this but another for me to make it for my son. I refused and did not pursue it.

Leviticus 18:21
Do not give any of your children to be sacrificed to Molech, for you must not profane the name of your God. I am the LORD.

As the days passed my ex became harder to handle. He constantly took me to court petitioning for more and more privileges. I had enough. Something rose up in me I had never felt before. The *spirit of anger entered.* That day I took a pail, all the photos I had of him, a cigar, some rum and herbs. I went outside and performed a ceremony. I had no idea what I was doing but the demon that had a hold of me did. I called upon my ex a marriage. I spoke that only sons would be born to him. I wanted him to leave mine alone, NOW! It was the most intense ceremony I had been involved in. I was not myself I was possessed. I finished what I needed to do and came back in the house. Two weeks passed and he came to visit our son. He then informed me he had met a woman the previous week and that they were getting married in a few months. I was amazed and my confidence was high. As he married he began to visit less and less and eventually had three sons leaving mine alone.

My powers grew and my confidence in the spirit realm became increasingly clearer. The next time I performed a spell of this type was for my cousin. She was in a physically abusive marriage and at the end of her rope. She was depressed and becoming sick. Her mother asked me if I could help and I said yes. I remember taking the sacrifice required. A black rooster covered in red ribbons. It was to be hung upside down at the edge of a train track. Within two weeks the husband left her and moved out of town. Wow! I thought, I am pretty good at this. Oh God how blind and lost I was.

Isaiah 44:9
All who make idols are nothing, and the things they treasure are worthless. Those who would speak up

for them are blind; they are ignorant, to their own shame.

There are so many areas in witchcraft which I studied that I can't recall them all. This stuff was really only icing on the cake. I knew that true power did not need all of this ritualism and stuff. Awareness that true power "believing you can, and so it is", was more real to me. So my search continued and focused on what I thought were more enlightened ways. New age mysticism, meditation, Yoga and so on. Focusing on the power of the mind and it's ability to create. Meditation was a way of life and spending an hour in total focus was easy for me. I participated in several groups and was growing in strength.

I remember on one occasion at one of our meetings, there was a hypnotist as a guest. He specialized in regression. That is when they hypnotize you and you go back to so called past lives. He went around the room asking questions for the purpose of finding a good candidate for the demonstration. I was it. While he was hypnotizing me, I recall feeling very comfortable and light as he was talking to me. I went back, back and then found myself in a dungeon. There was hay on the ground and fabric all over the floor. I realized that I must have been a seamstress by all that I saw. Suddenly an overwhelming grief came over me, a sense of no hope. I could not speak. All I could do was watch this person I was supposed to have been go through the life she had been born into. She was bound in this place and used in a manner of different ways. Her whole life was empty and I felt every emotion she was feeling. The hypnotist was in a state of panic. He couldn't seem to bring me back. His voice was far off and I could barely hear him. Slowly, by my own will I came out of it but not without stress. Do I believe in past life? I don't know. There isn't any proof that am aware of! What I experienced was real to me and I still remember it to this day. A vision produced by hell? Could it be the answer to what occurred that night? Or was I truly looking at my past life? Did I truly live in another century or was it that which was deep within me. Was I seeing what truly was in my soul? Could it be I was seeing the deepest parts of me?

My parents would occasionally go to these meetings with me. Nothing had changed. All I saw of their Christianity was their constant Bible thumping and their constant criticism of my walk. I thought it was ironic that they would quote the Word of God and yet also participate in the other. But then so did most of my psychic friends. They would take scripture and twist it to fit their beliefs. Most were good Baptists and a lot were Jews. My parents slowly departed from my ways into a more God centered life. They had become involved with strong ministries. Now they were determined to throw me in there with them, one way or the other. Of course this just pushed me further away. It made me resent and dislike all things Christian. What hypocrisy I saw! There was more love among the psychics, I had relationships with, than with the church.

Mark 7:6
He replied, "Isaiah was right when he prophesied about you hypocrites; as it is written: " 'These people honor me with their lips, but their hearts are far from me.

During this time I learned and grew in power and authority. I used it to help and do good, I never did evil to anyone. I taught others and therefore spread my knowledge. I had an altar to the saints. I worshiped them in my house where I would do my craft. Things such as herbs and food never perished while they were on the altar but as soon as I removed them they would decompose. It was real. This was the *spirit of idolatry*. In this period of my life I met someone that would influence me greatly. We will call her Rene. She also was searching for higher things and was learning as I was. We became inseparable. We did everything together. I became her guard in the spiritual realm we were functioning in. Many times I would have to go into the spirit and bring her back from dangerous situations. When she would go into a trance, she was defenseless against any attacks. That was what I was there to do, to protect. I became very proficient in spiritual warfare and in defensive strategies. Of course it was on the wrong side, but I have learned it works the same on the God side. With one big difference, "God always wins He is light."

Proverbs 2:7
He holds victory in store for the upright, he is a shield to those whose walk is blameless,

I was surrounded by three spirit guides that would help and teach me. And so entered *familiar spirits*. One who manifested as a gypsy. She would be the one who would speak to me when I did the tarot or gazed into the crystal ball. When she manifested around me I would change in my appearance and I looked like a gypsy. I remember on a Halloween night my dad's AA group was having a party and they asked if I would put a booth up and do tarot readings.

I made a tent at the corner of the Lutheran church's fellowship hall where they held their meetings. I was the gypsy that night, crystal ball and all. I was very busy that night. It is amazing how people, including christians, will submit to this kind of thing. All want a word, a prophecy, or a look into the future. Many came to me that night and all were amazed at my accuracy. Some left happy and some left in tears, as I brought to them their past and their future as I saw it before me. I never embellished and I always told them ahead of time that I would hold nothing back, not even death.

Another spirit control was an herbalist. This spirit would give me the recipes needed for whatever I was doing. Herbs and the combination of them are a very powerful thing. I have seen the mere presence of a particular plant make a person very uncomfortable. A certain tea given to someone can make them willing for suggestion. Many herbs are for healing both physical and spiritual. It is not something to be taken lightly. Several times I would witness as a bucket of water with particular herbs would expel a demon from within a person. Yes, it is true, a demon can be expelled by a non-Christian. The problem is that a bigger one will take its place. They don't leave without a greater motive or purpose.

The third spirit controlling me was the leader. He was to be my husband in the spirit. And he became such. He would guard me intensely. Anyone who would interfere with me in any way would feel his wrath. He was a constant companion. Later I will tell of my deliverance from him.

Many times I would awaken to things that looked like spiders floating over my bed. I have even been raped by spirits. During my Christian walk, through many counseling sessions with others, that spirit rape is more common than you think. On one occasion I remember one morning, I had gone back to bed while my son was watching TV. As I laid across the bed in my robe I felt a presence in the room. I couldn't move or talk. He then came towards me and laid on me and began to have intercourse with me. I remember to this day the weight of his spirit on me, the color of his hair, and the way his body felt. I knew I was awake but I also knew I could not move. My son came into the room to ask me something. The spirit stopped but did not leave. I remember telling my son I would be there in a minute. The spirit then continued and as quickly as he had entered, he left. It was as real as real could be. I was not dreaming. I had been raped!

Vampirism is another method they have of invasion. Yes, vampires do exist, although the real ones are spirit and don't walk around with fangs. They come in the night and take your life force, your energy. This is also very common.

I, being not afraid of the spirit realm, would just tell them to go away and they would obey most of the time. I knew I had authority and I used it very well. Even then, with all my power and abilities, there still was something missing in my life. There was a void I could not fill with anything I did. I knew there must be more, more and higher. My friends were all going in different directions and I was alone. Even my husband was far away from me. He never interfered with what I was doing and still doesn't. All he ever says is "How did it go and did you have a good time?".

I met a man at this time who was evil itself. He was very attentive and we would sit and talk for hours on end. He provided something I was in need of. We had so much in common. We both were interested in the occult and in mysticism. I found myself very attracted to him. Even then God had his hand on me and never allowed me to go further. The friendship dissolved just before it became an affair. I remember the night well, something in me rose up and said, "Run and don't look back." I did, and it was over, leaving me alone again with no one to share all I was seeing and hearing.

As I pondered and questioned, my eyes began to open and I saw the evilness around me. My friends began to do things that were wrong even in our psychic community. They would say that it was pay back, that the person they were hurting must have hurt them in another life. It was karma. So they would continue in their evilness. Even Rene, one I loved dearly whom I shared everything with and defended, was now moving on to evil things. She was doing things that I knew deep in my heart were wrong. I could no longer continue our relationship and I cried out to God. Here I was alone again.

John 3:19
And this is the condemnation, that light is come into the world, and men loved darkness rather than light, because their deeds were evil.

The Heart

Help me Lord for I am weary
There is a longing in my soul that tears my heart
Tears it in pieces and I see no healing for it
There is so much pain
So much loneliness in the world
So many walking aimlessly to and fro
Looking for peace
Looking for answers to questions
Oh! the questions
Those that no one can answer.
For only in the depth of the broken heart can the logic
be found.
Only there, can you truly see all that which destroys
and builds
The heart. It can be wicked and it can be good
Who can see?
Who can tell?
Can you repair the heart of man?
No!
Only He who created it can
He can destroy it.
He can repair it.
Only He can fix what man does to a heart.
Only He can fill the lonely places within it.
Only in the broken heart can you find.
The "One" who can make it whole.

3

A New Day

Psalm 3:4
I cried unto the LORD with my voice, and he heard
me out of his holy hill.

Yes, God! The Almighty, the One who knows all and is all. He heard ME! He moved me away from all things familiar. My husband got transferred and I landed in a little country town. I am talking about just one flashing light and that was downtown. My parents by now had given up on preaching at me and had focused on living the life before me as best they could. They tried to walk a stronger and more God centered life. They also moved to where I was and began to attend a little church in town. While in their house for dinner one time, I met their pastor and his wife. They had a true shepherd's heart. They did not judge me or preach at me, and instead they just loved me and we became friends. They allowed me to ask questions, and they never asked me anything. I remember we would talk and laugh for hours.

There, in this pastor's little church, I gave my heart to the Lord. It was July 24, 1983. I still, to this day, remember what I was wearing, how it felt and who was around me. I was born again and received the baptism in the Holy Ghost at that very moment. I began to speak in another language, the language of heaven. I was alone in a service full of people, no one saw or even noticed. I did! I will never forget when the Lord met me there. I thought that I had finally found my peace. Little did I know that this is when the true war began. For in me still were demons that had taken residence long ago. They were not going to leave so easily. I had belonged to them for a long time. They had become part of me.

Even though it was a Pentecostal church there was no understanding of the demonic realm. My spiritual house was not clean; no one had discerned that I was possessed. I had squatters on my land. My life now became a living hell. No matter how hard I tried to walk the walk, I couldn't. A year of torment began greater than I had ever experienced. I thought of suicide. I was as low as I could get. I would go out into the fields of hay and lay on the ground and cry for hours. Crying to God was only agony to my soul. He could not come near or hear me. He had found me only to leave me more alone than before. That is what I believed. I did not give up. Something in my deepest parts knew that it would be over soon. I prayed constantly. I studied the Word with such veracity I could have been considered mad. In doing so I came across a scripture that said they brought all their books on witchcraft and burned them.

"Acts 19:19 "
"And many of those who practiced magic brought their books together and began burning them in the sight of all;"

"That's it! That is the answer to my desperation." No one told me I had to get rid of all that stuff." So I brought all my books on the occult, my tarot cards, crystal ball, and papers. It was so much; all that I had gathered through the years. With my dear pastor present, I backed up my van, which was full. We made a pile and burned it all. There was a bon-fire at the church. The first in their history. As the fire blazed we took pictures, as a memorial of the event. Little did we know what we would capture in the flames. Many faces and figures of demons appeared in the photos. We were shocked to see all that was there. The crystal ball did not burn so the youth pastor who was a good friend took it to the nearby lake and threw it. We kept the photos and showed them to several people in the congregation. It stirred them to have another bon-fire where they brought all the things that were not pleasing in the eyes of God. It was an awesome thing to see. Much freedom was achieved for some. My dear pastor, later, destroyed all the photos. He was afraid of what he did not understand.

The torment however did not subside. I could not understand it. I would fast for days but felt no peace, only turmoil. God heard my cry.

Psalm 18:6
"In my distress I called upon the LORD, and cried
unto my God: he heard my voice out of his temple,
and my cry came before him,
even into his ears."

Hidden from me God had been preparing two women for the task. It took a year for them to come forward, for they did not understand. They questioned their beliefs, their dogma, and the way they had been taught and told how things were. They did not comprehend the possibility that a person who had given their heart to the Lord and spoken in tongues could be possessed. I was their first lesson, and they would learn it well. A year after my declaration and commitment to the Lord, on a Sunday night August 26, 1984, in that little sanctuary, the battle for my soul began. The war was fierce and the battle was long and difficult. I was not willing. "Why should I need prayer?" I don't need deliverance." I'm saved!" I said the sinners prayer, I pray, I speak in tongues and I read my bible. This cannot be!" But it can! I, like them, had believed what much of the church teaches. Once you have said the sinners prayer you are delivered and clean. NOT!!... Little did I know that in me were a group of devils, seven to be exact. Where they are, God is not. He wasn't able to take full charge of my life. I had to remove them from my domain.

As the night went on, one by one they were cast out and sent to the pit. These two women and I began to work as a team. One would read Scriptures, the other would give the commands in the name of Jesus and I would see the demons and if they left or not, how many and who they were. It felt like it took forever. They attacked me physically, they wrenched my back I was in such pain and agony I felt I would die. Later, I have learned that when the spirit of python leaves, it wrenches the back and causes much pain. Sometimes the pain never goes away. The demons even threatened to take my children and my life. I could hear and see them as they threatened me. They looked gruesome. Not at all the way they had showed themselves to me before. They were angry and willing to kill me. Several times I fell to the floor because I couldn't breathe. They were choking me. I would lay there twisted in pain. Crying from the agony I was in, my tears were so many my shirt was soaked. This was something I would have never volunteered to do. "The thief had come to kill, steal and destroy...John 10:10" We persisted till the end for there was no turning back. The last thing I remember is seeing a group of angels gathering the demons and taking them away in chains. It was over. I was on the floor on my back as I watched. I was tired and void of all feelings, empty but finally so clean. It was now time to finish it completely and seal it with the Holy Spirit. Gone were the spirits of unworthiness, rejection, fear, guilt, witchcraft python and many others I choose not to mention. But, there was still another battle....

Matthew 12:43-45
"When an evil spirit comes out of a man, it goes through arid places seeking rest and does not find it. Then it says, 'I will return to the house I left.' When it arrives, it finds the house unoccupied, swept clean and put in order. Then it goes and takes with it seven

*other spirits more wicked than itself, and they go in
and live there. And the final condition of that man is
worse than the first. That is how it will be with this
wicked generation."*

It had taken 7 hours. It was 3 in the morning by now. We were all so tired physically but spiritually energized. Then, God filled me fully with Him. I felt the peace I had longed for: that peace that no one can describe but has to experience. It felt like a warm shower after a long day of work. A word from the Lord came saying. " You are now clean and your gifts and talents are mine to use for my Glory. You have much responsibility, to whom much is given much will be required and I have given you much."

Luke 7:47
Therefore, I tell you, her many sins have been forgiven—for she loved much. But he who has been forgiven little loves little."

I now know that the devil goes to church, knows scripture better than we do, even speaks in other tongues and is very faithful. More, even, than some Christians. He goes to disrupt and to tempt, and to keep your mind on other things, and he is very good at it. So many times we bring him in with us, within our spiritual house. He had never been evicted. Many Christians do not believe this is true or possible. They are blind to the reality I experienced. No one can tell me that it was not true. No one can tell me that the demons were not in me. I felt them all, one by one, as they left me. I will never forget it. At that moment, I decided that as many people I could free from this torment, by God's grace and power, I would! Soon I would learn a hard lesson. Not everyone is going to believe you and you will always carry a mark upon your back. The mark of a whip that has been cast upon you by the enemy to make sure that those who do not understand, and are blind, will see it and fear. It is a mark that those of us who have been on the side of witchcraft, and new age stuff, carry. We see it on others who are still in bondage and we see it on each other. It joins us in a common bond. We are marked but now in the service of the King. We will be misunderstood and rejected. Even cast aside. That is something that our Lord endured and so can we.

Isaiah 42:6-8
"I, the LORD, have called you in righteousness; I will take hold of your hand. I will keep you and will make you to be a covenant for the people
and a light for the Gentiles, to open eyes that are blind,
to free captives from prison and to release from the dungeon those who sit in darkness.
"I am the LORD; that is my name!
I will not give my glory to another
or my praise to idols."

Thought for the day

Who can express the greatness of HIS being?
Who can imagine the wonders of HIS creations?
Who can phantom the many things
HIS hands have created?
Who?
No man can!
For man is limited in their existence.
He is only flesh made of dust.
Man can only ponder.
The flesh is unable to assimilate all that is.
Only in the Spirit can one hope to see.
Only in the Spirit can one feel.
Only in the Spirit can one attempt to touch the face of
GOD.
Only thru HIS breath, the RUAH.
Only thru the air that sustains our mortal flesh can we
be.
For in the vastness of all that is there is truly only
HIM.
Only GOD.
He is in all things and all things are in HIM.
HE is GOD.
There is no other.
HE IS.

4

The Road To God

So began a walk with God that was beyond words. I could not do enough, or be with Him enough. The more time I spent with Him the more I wanted. I remember times when I would go to the church after taking my kids to school and would sit on the floor with my head on the altar to pray. I would feel the Lord's lap under my face instead of the carpet. Those times were so intimate to me; so precious. Even then, it still was not easy. Though the devils no longer had a home in me, I had to get rid of and walk out old habits. These are the things left behind. Just like when you have a house and someone was allowed to live in it. You then decide that they are no longer welcome. So you evict them. They vacate but they leave all their stuff behind, their dust and trash. All the things they used and became comfortable with. Now you must fix the house. Slowly, one room at a time, repairs are made and rooms are restored. This was now my job. Two years after my salvation my beloved pastor went home to be with the Lord. He was a precious man and I still miss our talks.

Matthew 25:23
"His master replied, 'Well done, good and faithful ser-
vant! You have been faithful with a few things; I will

put you in charge of many things. Come and share your master's happiness!'

Few months passed and we welcomed a new pastor. It was hard to make the change. He was different and not as willing to embrace my revelations or opinions. Even though I loved him dearly, and learned much from him, troubles came. The devil was not going to give up so easy. He began to use brothers and sisters in the Lord to quench my flame. They would rebuke me when I used my gifts. They would tell me that I was a new creature and old things had passed away. Those gifts were of the old never to be used again. And so on....

There were many times, I would go to the pastor to tell him what I had sensed while sitting in the congregation. On one occasion, I discerned that a visiting family was in peril. The father was molesting his daughters. I came to the pastor with the information, as I knew I should, only to be told I was imagining things. Not! It was later discovered to be true. There were many such events, always confirmed but never taken seriously. In their eyes I was still marked. In their eyes I still carried the shame.

One Sunday, a friend came to me for some council. She was aware of my deliverance and was concerned about a friend of hers. She began to tell me how he would be one way and then he would suddenly change into someone she did not know. He had been involved in witchcraft and drugs but was now saved and going to church. She asked me if there was something we could do for him because he was being tormented. Oh, what hurt entered my soul.

I remembered my own time of pain. It was an over-whelming sorrow. "Why Lord? Why was he not cleaned at the altar when he first gave his life to you?" I told her I would pray and ask the Holy Spirit to bring him to the church. I remember telling her, the Holy Spirit had told me it was going to be on a Wednesday night. To this she replied, " He doesn't go to church on Wednesdays". I told her that if it was time for God to set him free, he would be there, and he would not even know why. I called the women who had minis-tered to me and we began to fast and pray.

Three days later it was Wednesday. She came running to the back of the building looking for me. I was at the time, working with the young girls' group. She found me and was so excited. "He's here, he's here, can you believe it he's here?" That is all she could say. Then she asked me to hurry because he wasn't in a real good mood and was fixing to leave. I told her not to fret, God brought him and it was his time to be free. As I made my way to the sanctuary, I prayed to the Lord that He would send angels to bind him to the floor and not let him go. I had so much faith then. I believed, as I always had, that all you needed to do was speak a thing with faith and it was done. I never hesitated. I never doubted. This would change.

Hebrews 1:14
Are not all angels ministering spirits sent to serve those who will inherit salvation?

I walked into the room to find the two women God had used to deliver me, waiting and they were ready. I looked and there he was. Crouched on the floor and getting very agitated. I saw the spirit within him and it had the resemblance of a werewolf. He could not understand why he was there and didn't want to stay but he couldn't move. He said there were weights on his shoulders. Yes, there were! Two large angels were holding him down. I came towards him and told him that God wanted him free and that we were there to help and pray for his release. He looked puzzled and had a wild glimmer in his eyes, something that I have seen before. There it was staring at me. That thing that held him captive.

We began to pray and ask the Lord for wisdom and discernment. The pastor then entered the room and inquired what was going on. We began to tell him what God had done in bringing the captive here. He then looked at him there on the floor, and asked him if he wanted prayer. The captive said, "No! I don't know what they are talking about. I am fine." What happened next was unbelievable. I saw the angels lift their hands and let him go. He got up and walked to the back of the room. He was no longer bound to the floor. The pastor, being the authority in that place, released him. The captive then turned away from the door and looked at us. What was looking back was the devil himself. The pastor turned pale and walked away from him. As the captive opened the door, he smiled as to let us know he had won. I was so angry and hurt. "How could you let him go. How could you!" I said. The pastor then said that we could not pray for someone that did not want it. I told him that when someone is possessed, there is no asking. The person has no free will. His will is owned by the devil. I didn't want a deliverance. I was not willing when I was approached by these women. We argued about it and I finally told him" Fine! When you find the scripture in the Bible that tells me that a demon possessed person comes of his own free will asking for deliverance, I will apologize to you in front of the entire congregation. If you can't prove this to me, we have nothing to talk about and the blood of this man is on your hands for tonight by the Holy Ghost was his hour to be free.

Ezekiel 22:13
" I will surely strike my hands together at the unjust gain you have made and at the blood you have shed in your midst."

I have learned much since then about anger. I now see that I was wrong in how I approached the pastor. As I was taught he was my covering and I was to be submitted to him in spite of my opinion, regardless if he was right or wrong. Needless to say, the apology never happened since there is no scripture. All demon possessed people came pleading to be left alone or brought by family or friends. None came of their own free will. I knew it from personal experience. I myself didn't want deliverance either. Not long before the year was over, at another church the captive finally was set free. Praise God.

This was the beginning of a journey that would slowly take my faith, my believing in the power God has given to me. I would be watered down. In my immaturity I would allow those who know little to speak into my life. They would bring death to my fire. Oh BUT GOD!

He is Great

Who can express the greatness of HIS being
Who can imagine the wonders of HIS creations
Who can phantom the many things
HIS hands have created
Who?
No man can!
For man is limited in their existence
He is only flesh made of dust
Man can only ponder
The flesh is unable to assimilate all that is.
Only in the spirit can one hope to see
Only in the spirit can one feel
Only in the spirit can one attempt to touch the face of
GOD
Only thru HIS breath, the RUAH
Only thru the air that sustains our mortal flesh can we
be
For in the vastness of all that is there is truly only HIM
Only GOD
He is in all things and all things are in HIM
HE is GOD
There is no other
HE IS

5

Gravel Under My Feet

Slowly my gifting was dampened and not used. It seemed that the space between my opportunity to minister grew greater and greater apart. I was resigned not to bother with that which was not welcomed. Many would ask for help and all I could do was point them in another's direction.

On one occasion, I brought a friend to a service given by a guest evangelist. He was known to flow in a deliverance ministry. I knew that she needed help. Her mother in-law was Jamaican and had put curses on her that had allowed demons to take residence. I hoped she could get free through this man.

There I sat with her as she became increasingly uncomfortable. The demons in her knew their time was coming to an end. The service concluded, he gave an altar call, and she went forward for ministry. As he laid hands on her she fell to the floor, out in the Spirit, they said. The ministry workers he had brought with him proceeded to pray for her and assessed that she needed deliverance. "Good!" I thought. Some shaking, and some moaning began. Then, suddenly, she was still. All was quiet. All those present began to praise God for her freedom. They clapped their hands in victory. It was a celebration.

I was sitting on the front pew not far from her as she laid on the floor. I knew deep in my spirit it was not over. The Lord then spoke to me and said. "Ok, now you go get it, you know it is not gone!" I argued with Him for a few minutes and reminded Him of my predicament with the church. He then said "Are you going to obey them or Me?" Well! What else is there to say? I got up and walked towards her. Some people around her, asked me what I was doing? Others said, "Isn't this great, she is free!" I looked at them and said, "No she is not!" "Oh yes, sister, don't you see how still and peaceful she is?" How blind, how wrong, what lack of discernment. I bent down and the Lord told me to put one finger, only one, on her belly. When I did, the power of God fell. She began to convulse, and there was such a scream coming out of her that people started to run out of the church doors in a panic asking what was going on. The pastor, of course, did not say that a demon was being cast out. He said that she was feeling the power of God. That was true. Oh! Yes, she was. After much shaking and screaming on her part, she got up from that floor clean and is still clean to this date. God had truly set her free.

Isaiah 49:9
"....to say to the captives, 'Come out,' and to those in darkness, 'Be free!' "They will feed beside the roads and find pasture on every barren hill."

This day I was confused. I was very confused. Why had God given me all this to then sit me on the pew? Why is the church not stepping out for the job at hand? There was another woman in need at the church I could no longer neglect. I called once again upon the help of those ladies and they came. We prayed for her and deliverance occurred but there was a new lesson to be learned. How far are you willing to go?. How much are you willing to give? How much do you really love? After the deliverance she was scared. She was not strong enough in her faith to keep them away if they came knocking at her spiritual door once more. Her wounds were still fresh and panic was setting within her. I asked God what to do and He said. "Take her home with you for three days." I had a spare room and so I did. Those three days I would learn that if the captive is weak they will fall again if not helped. This was a wounded soldier and she needed to be cared for till there was a healing. Three days and nights she stayed with me. The first night was a battle. The demons would come and wake her and torment her mind with threats. I didn't get much sleep that night.

The next day there was less activity. They are deterred by a busy mind and busy hands. Soon evening came once more and so did the tormentors. I finally took her and put her in bed with me so I wouldn't have to get up so often. This night the attack was more severe than the previous. Curtains would move without any wind. Doors would close and open by themselves. We would hear breathing and groans. There was a difference, though. I had the feeling they were being stronger not because they thought they were wearing us out but because they were losing ground. By morning of the second night, there was peace. The third night was quiet and she was strong. They never pursued her again.

As time went on, little by little, the devil accomplished his task. The women who had become my close friends after my deliverance, those women who had been with me through many prayer nights at the church, both became employed. They no longer could spend hours on Sunday night or any night praying at the church. I was alone most of the time. I no longer had someone to talk to whenever I wanted. They were busy with other things now. Being a new Christian of only four years, I submitted to the more mature Christians in the church, or so I believed. My joy was gone, my gifts waxed cold, and my life and walk with God became dull and a chore. I occupied myself with works that I thought would fill me. I was coordinator of the girls' group at the church. In charge of the social committee, choir member, cantata director, filled in for Sunday school when needed. Occasionally I took the place of the boys' group leader. On top of all that, I had a formal dressmaking business and was a wedding coordinator, cake baker, and provider for whatever else was needed. "Fill me, fill me!" was the cry of my heart. All those jobs, even though good, did not fill me. These works were empty.

Isaiah 57:12
I will expose your righteousness and your works,
and they will not benefit you.

Tired and lonely, the devil tempted me once again with the companionship of another. Many hours I would spend talking with him. He was a youth pastor. We both had a passion for the young, the children that we saw falling away. Again, I was faced with these feelings. Again I wanted so much to have a relationship with someone that would understand and would share my heart's passions. Again the Lord said, "RUN! And, take your hands off. Put your emotions aside. This can ever be. There cannot be an appearance of evil in either of your lives."

And so I did. I stopped all contact. It was a painful time, my heart was broken. Not because there was any thought of a sinful nature but because I would again have no one to share all the things that were in my heart. The youth pastor married and eventually became a full time minister. I had grown, and knew, there are lines we must never cross no matter what the cost is to us. I will never cross those lines. I listen to The Holy Spirit and He guides me. He is all the companionship I need.

Matthew 26:41
"Watch and pray so that you will not fall into temptation. The spirit is willing, but the body is weak."

During this time the church had grown and we bought the old school building. Much work needed to be done and if you have ever been on the building committee of a church you know that many battles are fought. What color the carpet should be. We had to decide whether or not to put this or that into the sanctuary. It was a very trying time, it was also a very exhausting one for me. We did a lot of the labor ourselves to save money and, as usual, ten percent of the church carries the ninety. All of our focus was on this building and God was set aside.

Finally, the day came that I broke down and I was burned out. I could go no further. No more was left in me. I called my pastor and told him I couldn't go anymore that I was empty. He said to me,"That's fine let us know if you need anything." That was the last conversation I had with him and I did not return to the church. I am not angry or do I hold offense for those at that church. They did not know what they were doing. All they knew was what they had been taught for so many years. They were set in their ways. I love them all dearly and we still keep in touch.

Psalm 31:9
Be merciful to me, O LORD, for I am in distress; my eyes grow weak with sorrow, my soul and my body with grief.

God in His loving kindness did not give up. There still was a little spark left in my heart that desired to go back to My Lord's arms and lay at His side. I wanted to see Him again, to go running in the fields where the breeze makes the blades of grass sing. There, where we so often met, and talked. I wanted so much to go back. I wanted to sit at His feet in the sanctuary and put my head upon His lap. I still longed for Him. He brought to my side a new Christian, even if for a short time. She had many questions and as I answered hers, mine were also answered. We began to search the Scriptures for the truth. God's truth not man's.

We would spend hours on end talking and questioning and searching for the truths that God has for all who are willing to find them. She helped me heal from many hurts imparted to me by the so-called believers that surrounded me. This was a time of wilderness. My husband had again been transferred and he had moved to another state while I stayed home waiting for the house to sell. I didn't even have a car. She took me with her to the church where she was now attending and I became involved in the choir with her. I loved that time of singing to my Lord. It was healing for me.

I met many loving people and became friends with the pastor. He loved my cooking. When there were guest speakers I would be called to prepare the meals. One of these guests was a well known, end-time prophet. He was there as our revival speaker. During the last service, while at the altar praying for someone, I felt a heaviness come upon me. It was as if a heavy blanket had fallen on me. It was like a blanket of fire. I began to weep not realizing the prophet had taken off his coat and had placed it on me. He was symbolically placing his prophetic mantle on me. Knowledge about impartations, or the passing of mantles, was foreign to me at that time. The importance and the effect this would have on my life would one day be revealed. I continued in that fellowship and experienced many things and had many visions.

I began to keep a ledger at this time. I began to receive words of prophecy for that church, for that pastor. This is one of those entries;

There are angels perched on the balcony listening and adoring as the Son of God looks down upon the man of God. The angels are dressed in luminous white, their faces glow with such brilliance it cannot be seen with carnal eyes. As they sit their hands sway in adoration to Jesus the Light for He sits on a cloud of such color it cannot be described. He looks down on His people and tears run down His face. He feels the pain they feel. He sees their lack of faith and can do nothing. As the people sing, a rain of Glory as tiny diamonds begins to fall and the higher the song the more the rain.

I was loved and was appreciated in that church for a short time. That would soon end.

1 Thessalonians 2:8
We loved you so much that we were delighted to share with you not only the gospel of God but our lives as well, because you had become so dear to us.

With time I have learned God uses me in some ways that cause me to get in trouble with man. It was morning and I was in my yard cutting the grass minding my own business. Out of nowhere I heard God say,"Go inside. I want you to write something down. I want you to deliver a message to the choir." I said,"Ok, when I get done here." Again He said, "Go inside and write what I want you to deliver to the choir". I said again "Yes Lord, I will, when I get thru with the grass." Well this went on for a few minutes and then the mower died! I should have known that when He says something, you better listen and do it.

Pronto!!! I went inside and began to write some Scriptures having to do with Love and the love the church should have for each other. I asked Him "What is all this about?" He said that the choir was out of love, there was much rebellion in it and He was sick of it. He then instructed me precisely how I was going to bring forth His word. I went to meet with the choir pastor and told him everything that had occurred and how God wanted me to do it. He agreed and gave me some time before the choir practice on a Sunday afternoon.

I left that day for church, still questioning God as to, why me? Why not the pastor? He only replied by saying, "Just do it." So I did. There I stood in front of 60 or more choir members. I, who had only been there a few months and had no intention to staying. I was there for only a season and a time such as this.

Romans 6:16
Don't you know that when you offer yourselves to someone to obey him as slaves, you are slaves to the one whom you obey—whether you are slaves to sin, which leads to death, or to obedience, which leads to righteousness?

There I was, standing before them, trembling. I told them to hold hands with the person beside them, as God had instructed. I then began to read what the Lord had given me. How He was sickened by the lack of love displayed for each other. How they had only concern for themselves. There were people there that were very allergic to perfumes and aftershaves. They were having to get up in the middle of service and leave sick because of it. They were being hurt by the lack of care and not only that, but the disobedience to the pastor. He had told them no perfumes or smells of any kind. This was a rule common to any choir. Some were not guilty but some were. People started repenting and weeping and I felt good, God had gotten through.

Then the unthinkable happened. One of the lead singers, the son of the church's prophet stood up and looked straight at me and said, " Who do you think you are? I'll be darned (he used a different word) if I am going to stop wearing my cologne for anyone. I spent a lot of money on it and only get to wear it on Sunday's. Those who are bothered need to be healed of their allergies or get off the choir!" I was not expecting that! My knees buckled under me and I fell to my chair. My weeping was deep and I was shaking so hard that I could not stop. The horror that came over me was more than I could take. He had just totally disobeyed God, not me but God! He should know better. This man that I loved to hear sing had grieved my Lord. He stormed off the stage and left.

2 John 1:6
And this is love: that we walk in obedience to his commands. As you have heard from the beginning, his command is that you walk in love.

Much happened to that church after that. The church split and the choir pastor left. I wonder sometimes if what happened that day was in some way the start of a purging. Soon after, my house sold, and I was able to join my husband. Another adventure in the Lord was about to begin.

My friend, the friend that took me to that church, sadly died of cancer a few years later. To this day I still wonder why. We prayed and fought with all we had and yet God decided to take her home. Sometimes I think she wanted to go. God has His ways and who are we to question the why. With time, my longing for our talks has lessened, but I still at times miss her very much. Throughout these years, I have had the opportunity to teach a few like her and in doing so I have learned a very important lesson. Someone once wrote,"A teacher teaches best what it most needs to learn." And I did learn. I learned to be careful not to give an opinion or try to teach something you have not experienced for yourself. God has a way of letting you experience firsthand your advice and opinions to others. I realized that my gifts of knowledge, prophecy, discerning of spirits, the authority I had to cast out devils, intercession, fasting and walking with God were no different than any other gift. Sewing, singing, playing the piano and a host of others, for they are also gifts given by God. If you once sang in a bar you don't give up singing; you do however, now sing unto the Lord. All of our gifts, some greater and some lesser but all gifts given by God are for His use and for His Glory. It has not been easy. Many things He has brought me through. My sons are now both grown and have a life of their own. They have their own walks and destinies to fulfill

Romans 11:29
for God's gifts and his call are irrevocable.

Life

What is life?
Only a mist upon the oceans of time.
Moving to and fro on the surface of this planet.
Life truly only begins when it ends
One space in time traded for another
Just as the tree dies and leaves the seed behind.
Only to grow and then in time die.
Also leaving its seed upon the ground.
Life therefore is what you make it,
Allowing the God of all things to guide.
For only He has the power,
Only He can change the course,
That you think you have made for yourself.

For without Him there is truly nothing
He and He alone truly holds time.
Time is in Him
He is time.
So don't fret, don't worry.
Stop striving to control what can never be controlled.
Who can control the Almighty?
No man, no woman, no power.
Rest in Him and He will do the rest
He will change the tides in your life
He will water the seed you leave behind
And tend to your garden
In the end it is all His.

6

Yet Another Place

I was now living in Georgia and in a new church. I thought that I would just sit and be still. It seems I never get to do that. My first encounter with the so-familiar demonic realm happened one December night. I had decided, after having been part of this church body for three months, to join the Christmas cantata. There I was quietly waiting for the practice to begin. A chill ran down my back. I looked at my mother who was sitting to my left across the aisle and she was already looking at me. She felt the same thing. I turned to see what had entered the sanctuary. A witch, it is a witch! I could not believe what I was seeing. I turned back around and tried to ignore her. After all I was once one myself. Besides I am not even a member of this church yet. It is none of my business. WRONG!!

She slowly walked up to the front and asked the choir leader if the pastor's wife was around. He said she was, and pointed in her direction. Panic filled my soul. All kinds of information was being dumped into my mind. I got up after a few minutes and found the pastor's wife. I asked her if she knew the woman and she said, "Yes vaguely." I then said, or better yet out of my mouth came "She is a witch!" The pastor's wife looked at me like a deer caught in headlights. She then replied "Yes she just told me that she had quit a coven and was inquiring about the church."

At the time this occurred to my pastor's wife. She was pregnant. I knew that witch was not here inquiring and I also knew she was still a witch. My fear soon was confirmed that she had come for the life growing in the womb. Two weeks later the baby was miscarried. Some would find this hard to believe and would say it was coincidence. Take it from someone who knows. It was not.

Job 24:14
When daylight is gone, the murderer rises up and kills the poor and needy; in the night he steals forth like a thief.

I was, within a few months, involved in all sorts of things. I decided to volunteer to help make some banners. I didn't know but a few people there, and the ones I did know, I had not known long. As I sat listening to this and that, a woman entered, who I will call Ann. She sat and began to give her opinion. I disagreed with her and that became the first of many disagreements. I didn't like her and she sure didn't like me. She was part of a counseling team there at the church. I found her arrogant and very opinionated. We didn't have much to do with each other. That was fine with me. This would soon change.

One afternoon the woman in charge of social things, who I will call Sue, asked me if I would be willing to give my testimony at their monthly tea. I guess I was fresh meat. I politely said no. I had vowed never to do it. I had given my testimony in Florida only to have it backfire. It had occurred during a Halloween night and we were having girls' meeting. They were all in their early teens. A discussion about why we were not celebrating this occasion came up. I tried to go around the subject but the girls were very persistent. So I decided to give them a small part of my testimony. They all received it and were now aware of the true meaning of Halloween. That was a mistake. All these little girls ran home and told their parents and they in turn told the pastor. Let's just say I didn't have them in my class again. So I kept my story quiet from then on.

I politely said no several times to this persistent woman. She was relentless. I finally said, " Fine I'll go to lunch with you and tell YOU. Then you decide if still it will be ok to share." Figuring she would hear and do as so many had done before, cut and run. Well she did not. Sue proceeded to schedule me for the next tea. I prayed and prayed that no one would show. I didn't want the scarlet letter on me so soon after starting this new church.

The evening came, and where there usually were 20- plus women only six attended. I was thrilled. I followed another short testimony with mine. I was surprised at the way I was received by these women. Ministry followed and a deliverance occurred. I was used again! However, it was different. I had never had a manifestation in my body after laying hands on someone. It took all I had to get home. I barely made it home as I was so sick in my stomach for a few hours. The bathroom was my place for a while. I didn't understand what happened till some time later. I had taken their junk into me and I didn't realize it.

2 Corinthians 1:7
And our hope for you is firm, because we know that
just as you share in our sufferings, so also you share
in our comfort.

Little by little I became involved in the inner circle of the church and worked in the office for a while helping with the tedious things like bulletins. One day Ann, the woman that I wanted to avoid, the one I just as soon not be involved with, heard about my testimony and came to ask me for help. It seemed that one of the women they were counseling was not getting anywhere and they thought that maybe I could discern the problem. They made the appointment and I was there. The girl was definitely full of stuff. All handed down through generations of witchcraft and control. I saw and reported and was given permission to continue.

One by one the chains on the girl were broken. It was glorious to see. She is to this day free and living for the Lord. Healed in body and spirit. From that day on I was called to the counseling room when there was something they could not get beyond. It became a regular thing. I recall on one occasion they called me in to sit on the session of this particular woman. She had lost her mother and her brother within a short time of each other. It had been several years and she was still mourning over them. She would constantly weep over their absence.

I sat in on the talk and then asked if I could say something. I was given permission to proceed. I looked at her and said,"What is your problem? Was your mom saved? Was your brother saved?"She said that they were. I then responded, "So this is the issue with you! You are just a selfish person. Why would you want them to be here? You are only crying for yourself because you are still here and they are not!" She looked at me and gasped. The look on her face was one of surprise but also relief. She then said, "You are right, and I never have been spoken to that way. I have never seen it that way." Then she thanked me and never again wept for the loss.

We became a team and many were set free through our obedience. Even I experienced another level of deliverance, which was that last stronghold. The demon who was made my husband in the spirit had been manifesting again. Maybe it was because I was becoming involved in the freeing of others. The devil doesn't bother with those who don't bother him. An appointment was made and there we were: me, the counselor Ann, the one who once I didn't like and Sue (the one who served me tea). My flesh felt as if it was on fire. I laid my head on Sue's lap and prayer was spoken. As it began the demon stood before me showing me the marriage decree signed by me and consummated by him. He told me it could not be broken. He lied!! God had a higher court and I had a greater decree. I was weeping deeply. Fear of this demon entered me. It was a deep battle only I could fight. I experienced something new this day. As I lay there I felt myself stand up in the spirit. I looked at him and took the decree from his hands. I tore it in two and as I did it burst into flames. I then took the ring off my finger (in the spirit) and gave it back to him. I felt a wind blow and he was carried away. I fell to the floor and was ministered to by angels. No more could he torment me. I belonged to a greater One. I belonged to Jesus.

Song of Solomon 6:3
I am my lover's and my lover is mine; he browses among the lilies.

I stepped into an armor-bearing role. I began to guard and minister with Ann. We did not go anywhere without each other. Time passed and warfare began in the church. There were assignments that needed to be broken and things that needed to be cleansed. We would go on Saturday nights and pray for hours walking the halls of the church. On more than one occasion apparitions would follow us out the door. Puppets would move by themselves in the children's church. So many things, it was hard to believe this was a church building and not a haunted house.

One evening we were praying in the pastor's office. We were without one at the time and were praying for discernment as to why the pastors were constantly being spiritually attacked and would fall or quit. As we prayed Ann went into the bathroom of the office. There had been a report of an apparition. She entered and looked at the mirror. She then looked around at the shower and suddenly began to shake and scream. "There is a black man hanging in the shower! There is a black man hanging in the shower." She kept repeating it over and over. She couldn't move or take her eyes from the shower stall. She was looking into the spirit. This had never happened to her before, she was overwhelmed and in fear.

"Ann!" I said, "You don't have to stay there. Give me your hand." When she did I saw all that had transpired in that place and why there was a curse on that land. I pulled her out, and after she had come to, I began to explain what I had seen. The land the church was on was part of a plantation. The man in the shower had been hung. I told her he was without a shirt and had calf length pants. His hands were bound behind him. His feet had been bitten by dogs. Ann said, "Yes that is what I saw." I then said, "He had been hung because he had had an affair with the lady of the plantation and she had become pregnant. All was fine till the baby had been born. It was black." He had been hung in her presence and left there to rot.

We needed to repent for this crime. Blood had been shed on this land and that is why it was cursed. We then went looking for Scripture to back it up. This is what we found.

Deuteronomy 21:22-23

If a man guilty of a capital offense is put to death and his body is hung on a tree, you must not leave his body on the tree overnight. Be sure to bury, him that same day, because anyone who is hung on a tree is under God's curse. You must not desecrate the land the LORD your God is giving you as an inheritance.

We repented making intercession for those who committed the crime. There were no more apparitions from that day on. So many times, Ann would be called in by the deacons to explain herself and the ministry. I would sit outside the door in prayer. She would be questioned and then would be asked if it was taken care of. I was there 5 years until I realized my work was done. If you are planted in the wrong field you will die. I was dying. The church was going in another direction. They were focusing on programs and good deeds. I had been there before. I wanted more than just good works.

Haggai 1:6
You have planted much, but have harvested little. You eat, but never have enough. You drink, but never have your fill. You put on clothes, but are not warm. You earn wages, only to put them in a purse with holes in it."

The land was clear and the curse lifted. In four years there had been four pastors during the curse but no more. New leadership was in place and is still there to this day. God brought the right person for that ground. He is a wonderful pastor and a friend. Even so, I could not stay. So I left and went to another church. Sue had moved to another town and for a while we would lose touch of each other. The counseling team I had become part of had also left a few months before me, and were at the church that I now began to attend.

God!

God! my God for I call for You in my deep hours
I call for You in the night when no sleep finds me
I call to You to rescue me and bring me to your side
Your side were there is rest from all this trouble that
surrounds me.
All this hurt that is infecting my spirit and soul.
Call for me and I will come for if You do not I cannot
enter your courts.
Cleanse me and make me pure so when you call I'll
be ready to see you.
I'll be ready to sit at your feet and rest.
Rest from the world and all its troubles, all its occupa-
tions,
all its lack of   direction.
Focus me on You Lord.
Let me see You. .
Put blinders on me so I may not see all the evilness
around me.
So I may only see before what You hold before me.
Hold me to the road You have planned for me.
Use Your rod and bring me back to it if I falter and
veer of the path You have set for me.
Call me, My Jesus to Your chamber
Call me to Your side.
Make me more hungry for You.
Help me put the worries of this world aside.
They are only distractions.
Keep me humble and meek before You.
Allow me to enter the throne room and come before
You.
Help my love for You, to grow.

Show me Your ways.
Show me Your ways so I may walk in them.
All the days of the life You have given me
May my love for You grow ever stronger
Hold me under Your strong arm and keep me
For I need You
I need You
Only You my King.

7

Many Trials

Ann and I became involved with women's ministries and saw many tangible manifestations of God. The power was so strong at our meetings that women would fall to the floor before even walking into the room. Even in the parking lot of the church, deliverance came to some. It was awesome. Women were set free some by the mere song that was playing. The men would come for prayer and receive healing. Miracles were increasing and we became known as the magnificent seven throughout the church. People knew that we would go at any time and any place to minister the freedom of God.

On one occasion, we were invited to a home group in another town. It was being held by my favorite tea drinker Sue. We went, and our leadership ministered the Word, followed by an altar call. God is so good.
Amongst the group was a woman in torment. As she came forward., I knew that this was demonic. I told a few that were with us to begin to pray and to stay out of it. I felt very protective of those who were immature. I laid hands on her and immediately we both fell to the floor on our knees. I was, in my mind, transported to the past where she had met with a witch during a trip to a nursing home. She had laid hands on the witch unaware of the demon living in her. He was looking

for another vessel since his was about to die. The demon had entered then, and I confirmed it with her. As I prayed and commanded it to leave in the name of Jesus, she gave out a scream and the force of the demon upon his exit, was so strong it knocked me down and pushed another one of the women there as it flew out the window.

Job 34:22
There is no dark place, no deep shadow, where evil-doers can hide.

During this time we met an apostle, evangelist, and prophet. We will call him John. Soon to be the son in-law of one of the women that attended the women's group. He was having a revival at a church nearby and we began to attend. That was the beginning of a friendship that at the time we did not know we would be under. He married and I was privileged to cater his wedding. As time went on and our friendship grew, our love for him and his wife increased.

The enemy however had an assignment against him. I remember one night, I attended the meeting alone. My friend Ann was away. As I sat there, I realized something was wrong. He was under the influence of something. I later found out that he was addicted to pain killers. I speak of this because it is not a secret. He openly speaks of it. I was very concerned for him and called Ann to tell her and to ask her to begin praying for direction. By morning we had our assignments. We were to tell him about our concern and we were to pray. Ann said she was to give him communion, and I would anoint him with oil. A very particular oil.

The oil, that was an interesting subject. I remember asking God what oil. "The oil you were given by the prophet" He said. This was oil that had been given to me by a mighty man of God. He was a member of a group of prophets who had prayed for, and imparted upon certain vials of oil. The Seven was what our group of women was called. We were each given one. I said, "But God there is so little." "All of it, use it all." He said. "You are to anoint his eyes to see, his ears to listen, his mouth to speak, his hands to do my work, his feet to go where I send him and then you will pour the rest over his head for a new anointing greater that he has ever had." I did as God commanded. We both did what we were told. Not without stumbling blocks and hindrances. I was determined that if we had to do it in the parking lot that is where we would do it. God is good his deliverance began and he was so full of God and walked in much power and spiritual authority, with a never ending hunger for more of God. I prayed it would stay this way.

Exodus 29:7
Take the anointing oil and anoint him by pouring it on his head.

Well, as you well know, the devil sure did not like what was going on in that woman's group. Again I saw the workings of hell as we were asked by leadership to stop all meetings. They had decided that there would be a book teaching and all groups were expected to participate. We asked if we could just add it to our regular meeting or do it another day. We tried to reason but there was none. We left. We did not want to bring division, but we knew that God was first and we had to obey the Holy Spirit. So we all departed and landed at a little church. We thought we had found refuge instead we found captivity. We were tired and weak and submitted to ceasing all activities. We agreed to just sit and do nothing. I believe that they offered this, hoping we would turn it down and not stay. Our reputation had preceded us and we were labeled as trouble makers. We were in a place of emptiness and wounding and so we submitted.

I knew this was God ordained. I previously had a dream and this church was in it. It was so detailed it could not be mistaken. The first time I drove down the street was like looking at the dream again. We were all amazed since I had shared it with the team. We decided that we were sent there and we should stay. As we tried to enter in, we were met with much opposition. There were several groups that functioned separately from each other. There was no unity and, as I sat and watched, I saw much demonic interference in that little church. The pastor had a spirit of anger and control.

As time went on it became apparent we were not wanted there. Only those who would be easily controlled were welcomed. Our stay lasted only a year. On a Wednesday before Easter, we were asked to leave. My dear sister and I were asked to walk out. We were told we had an unhealthy soul tie. I was called a witch. I was told that as long as I was with Ann she would never fulfill her destiny. There was so much hurt. I was told they were going to pray a fence around me so I couldn't influence anyone. I had no words to say. We were still in touch with John and he ministered to us. We had a long time of healing to go through and many things happened. So began my walk in the desert. This was my daily cry.

Psalm 63
O God, you are my God, earnestly I seek you; my soul thirsts for you, my body longs for you, in a dry and weary land where there is no water. I have seen you in the sanctuary and beheld your power and your glory. Because your love is better than life, my lips will glorify you. I will praise you as long as I live, and in your name I will lift up my hands. My soul will be satisfied as with the richest of foods; with singing lips my mouth will praise you. On my bed I remember you; I think of you through the watches of the night. Because you are my help, I sing in the shadow of your wings. My soul clings to you; your right hand upholds me. They who seek my life will be destroyed; they will go down to the depths of the earth. They will be given over to the sword and become food for jackals. But the king will rejoice in God; all who swear by God's name will praise him, while the mouths of liars will be silenced.

Lord where am I?

The feeling of a vast emptiness before me.
The desert of the soul is around me.
Yet I feel, in the depth of this void, your hand.
It holds me gently as I walk.
I walk, eyes closed, only trusting in your gentle touch
I move to and fro as you lead.
With no knowledge of the destination you have for
me.
My trust in you alone keeps me from fretting.
For I know not what the future holds.
You keep it from me, so only in you can I trust.
Only You know all things
Only You determine the outcome of my life.
Only You have all things in Your hand
It is for Your purpose I live and breathe.
It is for Your purpose that You have created me
Only to worship and adore You
To blindly trust with no other expectations
Only to please You, the Lord of all things
Carry me Lord, forward in Your loving hands
Soon I will be in Your presence
Soon will I stand before You
But until then, my Lord hold my hand.
Don't ever let go
Without You I will be lost
Without You I am not.
Without You my life has no purpose
There is nothing or ever will be anything without You
For You are the forever

8

In the Desert

My walk in the desert was not very long but it was very painful. There was much I needed to learn and much that I needed to dispose of. There was also much I needed to walk away from. A year after our dismissal we were invited to a home church where the power of God fell and healing was brought forth. Words were spoken over me and my dear friend. We left that place free of all that had been placed and spoken over us. I continued to fellowship there. For a time so did Ann, but that quickly changed. She began to disagree with the man of God at that place. She slowly stopped going, however, I could not. God was doing something in me. There was something for me to do, something to learn. So I would go alone.

By now we had been also attending John's home church meetings and so we were beginning to become active again. A pastor near my house had called and asked us to start a prayer meeting at his church and so we did. Those prayer meetings were powerful and a place where I went even deeper in the things of God and in the workings of spiritual warfare.

On one particular evening, we had several people at the prayer meeting. One lady in particular had come for deliverance. She had been battling prescription drug abuse. There was a demon in her flesh that kept her from reaching the victory. As the evening began she became exceedingly uncomfortable. She started to tell her husband that she needed to leave. She didn't feel well. That, to me, was great. The demon in her was stirring and making himself known. They brought a chair to the middle of the room and asked her to sit. She reluctantly did, and so began the battle. I, during deliverances, never step up or touch unless God gives me permission. It is something that I have always done and wish others would.

Prayers got loud and commands got louder. The woman was crying. There were some people yelling in her ear telling the demon to leave. Nothing was happening. I was in the corner of the room with my back to all the commotion trying to discern why it was not leaving. Ann kept looking at me and motioning me to come. I could not. God had not released me. Then, suddenly, at the peak of all the noise and voices, God whispered to me, "Tell them all to hush. You go and whisper for it to leave. There is no need for noise and loud voices. The level of noise does not determine the level of authority."

So I turned around and just whispered, "Shshshshshsh," motioning all to be quiet. They looked at me in puzzlement, and stepped away from the woman. I slowly came towards her listening to God's whispers. There she was. Crying uncontrollably her face reddened from the strain she was in, slumped down in the chair. I leaned over and said in her ear. "You know who I am. I come in the name of Jesus, and in His name, and by His authority, come out." She suddenly gave a yell as if someone had pulled her guts out. She then slowly fell to the floor and was free! I was amazed, I was so excited. I had reached a higher level of authority. There was no need to yell only the need to know your place in God.

Matthew 9:8
When the crowd saw this, they were filled with awe;
and they praised God, who had given such authority
to men.

Stress began to occur between Ann and me. There were discussions and arguments and many differences of opinions. She did not understand why I would go and do things without her even though she didn't want to do them with me. I felt her intent was for me to do what she felt I was to do. I began to resent her, and friction was created.

During this time as we were growing apart, her husband became ill and it wasn't long before he went to be with the Lord. This was the beginning of the end. I had gone to another state on family business the night he fell ill. She needed me and I felt guilty because of previous commitment I could not be by her side. I could not change my plans and this was stressful for her. When I returned, I moved in with her during her husband's final days. I loved her and didn't want her to go through this alone.

I would get up in the middle of the night to give him his medications. I would help her with his care during the day. As he worsened, he was blessed with wonderful hospice and this was a great relief. Much needed to be done, many preparations and decisions, and I stood by her side through it all.

Proverbs 18:24
A man of many companions may come to ruin, but
there is a friend who sticks closer than a brother.

Soon after he entered hospice, he died and a new chapter in her life was about to begin. All those things required were done and two months had passed. I made plans to go on a short trip with her and two other friends. At first she didn't want to go but ultimately she did. We all needed a rest.

I will never forget that trip. We missed our road exit. Then we were rear ended by a truck. Thank God no one was hurt. The van was now without a rear window, and it was raining. Plastic and tape fixed the problem and we continued to the hotel. At the time, I didn't realize how prophetic this event was. I was the only one in the car that had a rear view mirror and saw the truck coming. I saw it coming. There, at the beach, the end of our 10 year friendship began. Ann informed me at breakfast that I had been replaced. I was shocked not knowing what to say. There I was, three days left before going home, and in the middle of a tropical storm. Both in the natural and in the spirit, I was hurt. The deepest parts of my soul had been ripped out and trampled underfoot.

We got back home and things got worse. I couldn't forget her words to me. I couldn't stop wondering what I had done to merit this. I felt she began to question my comings and my goings. It seemed to me that she became even disagreeable about me attending the home church even though it never interfered with my taking her where she wanted to go.

Slowly it became unbearable. However God had a plan and I willingly laid my life in His hands.

Deuteronomy 22:10
Do not plow with an ox and a donkey yoked together.

We had become unequally yoked. We had an unhealthy soul tie. Her ideas and mine had, and were, growing farther and farther apart. I continued with the home church and growing within. Much revelation was imparted to me and much discernment. I was hurting. My heart was broken and there had begun a manifestation in the flesh. I was in much physical pain. I didn't know that it was related. It was spiritual and I would go thru much. Freedom was soon to come. During this time, many prophetic words were spoken over me. And I kept them all in writing and in memory.

Time was passing and I began to relax. Things seemed to lessen. Ann became more agreeable. I continued going to the home church and she even began to go with me again. Things seemed to be as before but deep in my spirit there was a hesitation. I felt as if the roof would cave in on me at any moment.

Late one evening the Lord came to me with a message, "Oh no God not again! I can't do this again," was my complaint. He had a word for the pastor over that little home church. He was a man with much anointing and discernment. A man deeply troubled with things from his past. Places he had been and ministries that he had been involved with that were cultish. I knew of his troubles and I had prayed with him many times, always just skimming the surface. Never going for the deep stuff.

God knew I would hesitate but He also knew that I would go. He told me that I needed to approach him as Nathan approached David, with much humbleness and very low. I was to present the situation as if it was someone else I was talking about and then ask his opinion as to what to do. I did as commanded and sitting there before me he recognized his trouble. He recognized he had been killing his own sheep. He wept and asked for ministry. We were there for an hour, me, his associate pastor (who was aware of the situation), and him. We ministered to him and there was much accomplished. Yet the root was still there. It was not to be handled at this time. I knew that soon it would rise up and strike. It was a fearsome adversary within him. I knew it would probably be me it struck.

Ecclesiastes 12:14
For God will bring every deed into judgment, including every hidden thing, whether it is good or evil.

This man had several personalities, all very aggressive, rude and controlling. All but one. That was the real man. That was who I so wanted the Lord to free. Very seldom I had been in the presence of this personality. This was one of those days. I had gone to minister as I usually did on a weekday. After ministry, he asked if I had eaten. I said, "No," and so we left and got a bite. He was polite, focused, not at all scattered, as usual. I was able to have clear conversations with him, and I even got a lot of background information. I heard stories and accounts that confirmed what I had suspected on how the demons had gained access. There were plans made to serve communion on Sunday and when we returned to the house, I helped get all ready for it. We parted that evening and all was fine so I thought.

Again, I would be asked to leave. Again, I would face the pain of being rejected. My welcome at the little home church did not last long. I was sent by God to deliver freedom and was not received. After almost a year of fellowship and ministry, I was asked to leave. The enemy doesn't like it when he is discovered and his territory threatened. This is a war we are fighting. Many receive the help the Lord sends but many are blinded by their ideas and misconceptions. Many are misled by demons that have become so ingrained in them they don't even know who they really are.

Matthew 15:14
Leave them; they are blind guides. If a blind man leads a blind man, both will fall into a pit."

There I was sitting, with my spiritual daughter, one Sunday afternoon at a restaurant before the service, when phone rang. I saw it was the pastor, so I answered it. As the conversation began I was filled with shock and grief. I was brutally asked to leave the group. I knew that I had an assignment. I had always known that God had sent me there and much had been done but the last battle was about to be fought and that was never to be. The enemy's stronghold was too great. The enemy won this one. The captive would not be freed through me.

I immediately called the assistant pastor and told her what had occurred. I told her my fears and all I had discerned. She was also in shock and didn't want to accept that this was going on. She had a home church of her own and her license was through his ministry. She could lose much. At first she hesitated to believe all I told her and all God had revealed to me. I finally told her that I could not convince her. She needed to seek the answers herself. I told her that I would be praying for her and I would be here if she needed me.

I learned a lot from them and received words of prophecy confirming much that God had spoken to me. I took from there a captive and she is now a daughter in the Lord. I don't fully know what God planned for me there, but I do know I was obedient. Throughout this I became more free to be on my own which is something I struggle with. I needed to learn to stand trusting in God and Him alone.

Sadly to say, not long after my departure that little home church fell apart. There is no one there and all foreign ministries were severed. He had been over several churches in Ireland and Germany. There, the man stands with the stronghold he would not give up. It saddens me so. There was so much potential, and so much promise. The associate pastor finally saw all I had said for herself. After several attempts to get him help from others, she separated from the ministry. She is now on her own and her church is growing. We have kept in touch.

Gory in the Gloom

Out my window I look and see.
The day is gray and cold.
But even among the grayness I also see,
Birds flying about doing their daily shores.
Singing their praises, as they fly to and fro.
They are not bothered or deterred,
by the gloominess around them.
As if they could see beyond the veil of gray
into the blue sky on the other side.
They go about their daily shores.
They don't worry if it will stay.
They know what is on the other side.
And that soon as the sun rises.
It will burn all the fog away.
Then the brightness of the day will appear once more.
Could it be so simple.
Could it be so plain.
That if we would do as the birds do.
And also would sing praises to the King.
Even in the midst of the grayest day.
Even when we don't see beyond the veil.
We sing praises to the King knowing that the blue sky
Is just on the other side.
And as the Son rises with our praises.
The gloom of our darkest day will burn away
Then the sky will shine once more
Clearly to show the Glory of our King.
And the love He has for all those
That sit so happily under His wing.

9

The Healing

Nine months of testing and burning in the refiners fire had passed and I was asked to go to a retreat with a friend who knew what I had been going through. I had gone to her church on two occasions to minister with the team I had been involved with so I was familiar with a few of the ladies who would be there. This is what occurred there. It is a very small part of all that went on at the retreat. There was so much more that God did. I am not able to recall it all.

After being picked up by that old friend with the tea habit, Sue, we arrived at the camp site. There were cabins with a large commons room in the middle of the area. I was very glad to see the improvements to this location. We had been there previously when we were attending the church we met at and that place was not as nice as it was now.

We continued to unpack and get ready for the rest of the leadership women to arrive. It was 2 p.m. and they sat to discuss the schedule. I listened as they realized that it was not going to go as planned. The Holy Spirit began to change it all, and I was amazed at the fact that they were allowing Him to do so.

A few days prior, I had been asked for some suggestions. I mentioned to Sue, when she told me what the theme was, that they should have communion. I felt the communion should not be the usual. It should be a communion of intimacy. A communion where they take the body and the blood into their bodies as in becoming one. This is like in a marriage and it should be a honeymoon night communion. She agreed and told me to bring everything necessary and I would be doing it. I protested and told her that I was there to clear my head. I was there to rest and be alone with God. I needed to find myself again. This was the tea woman. She is very persistent. Well, as I sat there and listened to them work things out with God, I began to get nervous. After all, I didn't know these women. I was only there to use a bed. I began to pray and tell God, "It is up to you I have nothing you don't give me. So here I am."

Deuteronomy 11:1
Love the LORD your God and keep his requirements, his decrees, his laws and his commands always.

They finished the schedule and what they then called "tentative"   could change at "a moment's notice". Well, they got dinner moving and told me that I should go out to the campfire site and get it going. Good thing I know how. There would be a testimony, and after it communion. I agreed and got things ready. The Spirit of God had begun to move and there was an expectation in the air. I spent the afternoon praying and just being quiet. It was wonderful.

As it got dark I proceeded to the campfire with the woman whose testimony we were going to hear. They all arrived shortly thereafter and took their seats.

It was a beautiful night and the moon was full. The testimony began. It was awesome! I can't remember all the details but I do remember the fact that she died and then went to heaven. She described what she saw in heave, as tears ran down hers and many other faces, including mine. She confirmed things I had seen and or felt myself. She talked about how many people she has run into that have had experiences similar but never spoken about them. It was just amazing. Sue then spoke about how she had shared the experience with her before she flew to Florida and it had an impact on her. You see she was petrified of flying. Not this time, even though the flight was not good. There was a drop that caused people to fall out of their seats. People were screaming and so on. Even through all that, she had no fear. She had peace in knowing she would go to the place the one who had died had gone. Both testimonies were incredible.

Revelation 12:11
And they overcame him by the blood of the Lamb,
and by the word of their testimony; and they loved not
their lives unto the death.

It then came to me and I passed the communion to all and prayed. I can't remember what I said. I do know it was God. The Holy Spirit fell and women were on their faces. Ministry began and I stepped away since I felt that they would like prayer from those they knew and trusted. Well, I was wrong and they began to come to me. I prayed for some, imparted to some and God delivered one. The deliverance was one that I won't forget.

I had prayed for her and talked to her for a little while and then it was revealed. She began to twist and bend back like a pretzel. It took three women to get her to the ground without her falling into the fire pit. All I was doing was softly saying what the Lord was telling me. I was not loud or forceful. It was amazing. It looked like something from a movie.

After a few minutes she ceased her contortions and sounds and was still. The Lord then told me, "That is enough for now". As I took my hand off her stomach it felt as if I was being unplugged from a light socket. I fell to the ground on my knees with an overwhelming feeling of awe and wonder. Sue came over and prayed with me as I shook with God. This was the beginning. I was beginning to be free to be what God wants from me.

Psalm 119:45
I will walk about in freedom, for I have sought out your precepts.

We left the site and walked back to the commons room and ate again. I was so hungry. We sat and talked for a while and women were coming and asking me what God meant by this or that. They were so hungry for more. By the time we were through fellowship it was 11:30. I got a shower and cried, not because I was sad but because of God's magnificence. Sleep did not find me. I spent the night praying. Even in the night, God worked miracles. Sue had mentioned that she was having problems with her bladder and with her voice since her trip to Florida. During the night, as she slept next to me and I prayed, God healed her of both things.

Psalm 143:1
Hear my prayer, O LORD, give ear to my supplications: in thy faithfulness answer me, and in thy righteousness.

Morning came in as a flood. The breeze was warm and you just knew that God was there. You could just feel it everywhere, as I sat there on the bed with Sue looking for scriptures to compliment what he was going to share in the afternoon session. Out of my mouth came "Why are you fretting? You are not going to need any of what you are doing." She just looked at me and replied that she wanted to be ready. Breakfast was given and the morning teaching began.

The first speaker taught on Mary and Martha, a teaching very familiar to us all. It was on how we need to be both. She sat down and then the pastor's wife came to the podium. She stood there for a while and suddenly fell to the ground on her knees. As she lingered we began to pray and I heard her say my name, "Put some music on,"she said. That also became my duty during this retreat. God had told me to bring all my CDs and I had. Well, I guess He knew they would be needed? Hmmm. Well, I got a word for her. I had no idea what it meant or why but I got down on the floor with her and whispered in her ear what the Lord told me. She instantly began to weep even deeper. I guess I heard right.

Women began to speak in tongues and sing. It was Holy Ghost pandemonium. Those who didn't have tongues were asking for hands to be laid to receive. Some received healing and some were refilled. It was just crazy. Women laid out all over. This went on for three or four hours.

The lady who had deliverance at the fire got some more. There were young women, there were old women and all in between. It was incredible. They were all ministering to each other as the Spirit moved. God finished what He was doing for that session and my friend did not need all she prepared for, after all.

Mark 13:11
Whenever you are arrested and brought to trial, do not worry beforehand about what to say. Just say whatever is given you at the time, for it is not you speaking, but the Holy Spirit.

While we waited for lunch, I sat out on the porch and pondered the wonders that were happening. The woman who had died arrived from court where she had proceedings that morning. She was being sued and was going to lose some land she owned. As she passed by, I asked her how it went and she told me not good but that after her experience in heaven she knew that all things are in His hands. I sat and my heart hurt with compassion. It was not right what these people were doing. I remember saying, "God she is your child. Let her enemies be scattered and let them fall at her feet." I then saw her on the phone and she began to shout that the people were going back to the table. Something they said they would not do. It was not even 20 minutes later that the call came in. They settled in her favor! I was in shock with my hand on my mouth and all I could do is remember my apostle, my covering, saying not long before while he prophesied over me, "The scepter is outstretched and whatever you ask up to half of my kingdom will be granted." I didn't know what to say or think. I know we have authority but do we really realize how much? I sat there with tears flooding down my face. Why me, God?

Ephesians 6:18
And pray in the Spirit on all occasions with all kinds of prayers and requests. With this in mind, be alert and always keep on praying for all the saints.

We had lunch and decided to have free time the rest of the afternoon. Some went to their rooms and took naps, while some just sat and talked. My group took blankets and music and laid by the lake. We did not speak we just soaked in the Glory of God. We were there for three hours. It was so good just to be quiet before God and let Him love on me.

Dinner was at six and then the evening session. Darleen was next on the agenda. She also had a testimony that everyone should hear. Hers was on how God had healed her of a disease that made her allergic to everything. The doctors wanted to put her in a bubble. She was sick for seven years. Then the Lord came in and began to deliver her from fear. That was the cause of her allergies! She spoke on the fact that it wasn't over night, but that it was a process for her. That just like in base ball, there are different ways to get a home run. So there are different ways to get a healing. After she finished she called for those who needed healing and The Spirit began to minister.

During that time I had been out under the Glory of God. He spoke to me and told me that there would be three deep deliverances and that there would be 7 promotions. I said, "Ok." I knew of one of the deliverances (the woman at the fire) and he gave me the name of six of the promotions. He wouldn't give me the 7th. I figured He would give it to me later. These names or faces were not who I would have chosen, but then it was not my choice was it? He gave me direction and I waited for the go ahead.

As ministry continued, I waited for God. He told me not to announce that there would be promotions for it may not be understood by the young of spirit. I was to just go to their ear and tell them they were promoted and in what area He was promoting them. I did as He asked. One by one I gave what He spoke.

One of these women was a very quiet, meek woman. Almost slave like. Her mother was with her and this young woman was at every beck and call to her mother. I noticed this because I was amazed that she would not even sit before her mom would ask her for something else. As I went to her and told her that God was promoting her, she fell to the floor. I then went down to her ear and began to tell her that God was releasing her and that she was a slave to no man. She was to love her mother but she was not to be her slave. She was free to be a servant to Him. She began to shake and cry and then suddenly she got up and started jumping uncontrollably and laughing it was to the point of disrupting. Sue came to me and asked what I had done and I told her that I didn't do anything, God did. But Sue said she was being a disturbance and for me to make it stop. I understood and so did God. They were not ready for this yet. I went over to her and put my finger on her forehead and said, " BE Still and REST." She fell out again and stayed there the rest of the service. WOW it was so cool.

The problem I felt was that people were looking in amazement at me and that was something I did not want. I continued to minister and others came for freedom. I knew there was one more deliverance. One deliverance God had revealed to me. She and I had already talked about it and she knew it was coming. It was time and The Lord sent for her. She was to be delivered of deep anger and resentment (go figure) Darleen was at my side and we began to pray for her. Then, God directed me to lay my hand on her belly and a scream that seemed to take forever came out as she fell to the floor then, there were two more and it was done. She felt it and she knew it. She was free and God refilled her with the fight she once had. His fight. She is a prayer warrior again.

Of all the promotions I knew that the 6th one was going to be pastor's wife. It was getting late and I still had not gotten the 7th. So I thought that perhaps it is for someone tomorrow, so I continued. By now there were only 6 of us left. I began to pray for the pastors wife and impart what God was saying. As I finished, one of the women that was there praying with us came up to me and whispered in my ear, " YOU ARE BEING PROMOTED!". I was the 7th! I fell to my knees weeping and was just overwhelmed. This was just more than I could ever imagine. God is just more than more magnificent.

We all retired and went to bed. By know it was 2 AM. Sleep did not come. I was just so full. My mind could not be still just reliving all that had happened to the women on this trip. We arose and had our last meal together followed by a time of reflection. One by one they began to speak and one by one I was blown away at the fact that I was an instrument for what they received. One that stands out was the woman that we know lovingly as "tiger". Can you guess who? Well, she was still smiling and jumping out of her skin. Her mother spoke and said how God had healed her during the night of pain that she was in due to a surgery she recently had. She stood up and touched her toes and twisted at the waist. She was not able to do this before. Then, her daughter, "tiger", jumped up and said she had also been healed. She was diagnosed with severe asthma that was going to require her wearing an oxygen mask. SHE WAS HEALED and could breathe! I later realized that when God set her free, He set her free from what was taking her breath. She was being choked.

I then shared with them that this was the first time I had ministered in such a way without Ann at my side. There was so much more I can't even remember it all. There were so many questions asked of me. I felt like a buffet with all these people just wanting more.

Acts 14:17
Nevertheless he left not himself without witness, in that he did good, and gave us rain from heaven, and fruitful seasons, filling our hearts with food and gladness.

We departed that place and were a little sad. I prayed that all that was done would stay and grow in all of our spirits. Sunday came and we were there at 8 AM for prayer with the Pastor. The women who were at the retreat were on fire. It was so thick you could cut it with a knife. Pastor had a hard time keeping himself from jumping all over the sanctuary. The first service was electrifying. They hold two services on Sunday morning. When the second began it was nuts. The revival they had been praying for had landed. There were men at the altar crying, women screaming and healing happening. It reminded me of the time I went to Brownsville. God showed up and they did not stop Him. It was great!

I don't know what God is doing with me or what I will be doing for Him. All I know is that there is a burning in my bones that I don't want to quench and a hunger I don't want to satisfy. I want more, and more, and more. I want to pass it on, so all around me get the same hunger I have.

I know that I said awesome, wow, amazing many times. Well, there are no words on this planet to explain what happened. I am sure that there are places where this is common. It is not common here. I never want it to become a routine. I never want it to stop being amazing and awesome.

Thursday, at the beginning of the retreat as the power started to increase, I began to have a nose bleed. Then, as Sue was praying for people with me, her nose started to bleed. I remember that we were at a service, with my apostle, where the power was so strong and he got a nose bleed. I also woke on Saturday night with a blue mark like four fingers on my leg. This was after I had prayed for those deliverances. Hmmmmmmm.

HE IS

" HE IS the Almighty, Worship Him"
" HE IS the Only God, Worship Him"
" HE IS the Strong Arm, Worship Him"
" HE IS your Salvation, Worship Him"
" HE IS your Healer, Worship Him"
" HE IS your Deliverer, Worship Hm"
" HE IS"
Worship Him in Spirit and in Truth
Worship Him with all you are and all you have!
Worship Him!
Him, Alone, and Only
No other is Worthy
No other is He.
Worship Him!

10

Are You Willing To Die

During the year after the retreat many things happened to me. There was much pain, and much hurt. The rift between Ann and me became greater and deeper. There was no hope for reconciliation, for now. Our paths had become different and our yoke was not equal. There is nothing I can say except that part of me died. That person that once was, is no more. I laid my life down to be stripped of all that was familiar and safe for me. I was put on the threshing floor to dry and then was thrown up into the wind of the Holy Spirit, where all that was "not to be," would be taken away.

had to turn my back on someone I loved with all my heart. I had to walk away. Much was spoken. Many accusations and hurtful things were said. Many who were once friends were no more. I had a different road ahead. Advice was given and followed. Looking back I should not have taken. God had a plan.

This chapter is short and there is no more. For no more can be said about what occurred between her and me. At the beginning of my dying, a prophet of God spoke these words over me. At the time they did not make sense and I didn't feel they applied. I was wrong.

"My daughter the time has come for the reckoning of peace for My sake. For I have raised the up in the midst even of this generation, I've raised the up be-

cause My heart has been manifested in your heart and even your ways says the Lord. But I would seek that ye come after peace as never before. The peace that passes understanding, that goes beyond the obstacles of life. Even My river of peace from were you have drawn your strength and your power, and all that is of me, you have found in My river of peace. But know that there are those who would rip, that would tear and that would sow discord even in thy spirit for the sake of their own iniquities. For they will not reckon themselves unto me. I have placed the even in the middle of my river says the Lord, wherein I do stand. Know that the turbulence shall increase in moments, in hours, in days, in weeks, in months and in years. The seasonal tracking of those who walk in My ways will be changed by this time next year. Know that I've called you to be in the midst, says the Lord, even in the middle. So know that my peace must reign. Know that those that sow discord within your spirit are those that I will lay aside in the coming hour. If they do not seek Me with all of their hearts, says the Lord. For you have served well but have not been served. You have submitted your ways unto Me amid those who refuse to submit their ways unto Me. For I would not have you sown and planted amid discord. I would not have your life sown and planted in a river mixed with man's ways in the world. For those who seek man's ways and the world's ways have no ears to hear and their eyes in this hour are growing dim. For they are not prepared as the eagle to gaze into the Son. For the Son of righteousness has come with healing in His wings and rested His anointing of healing and mighty deliverances upon you. But you have not cho-

sen to rest yourself, and you are finding unrest, not because of that wish is in thy spirit but because of those that would rip and tear asunder, drawing you away from My purposes and My calling for thy life. Know that I am in the midst of thee and I will cause a turning. I shall indeed cause a turning that you will witness with your own eyes. And you will say why, why, oh why did not these people turn unto you. And you will have the propensity to grieve for them. But know that I have already grieved. Thou shall take the grieving elements and place them upon Me and I will raise you higher than you ever dreamed. For My will and My ways shall be accomplished in thee, My daughter. They shall indeed be accomplished. Know that family and friends that choose to walk in their own ways shall be bypassed from the realm of the new anointing that shall destroy not only old yokes but new ones. For even my people have yokes themselves to that that was not dispatched. And My people have yoked themselves in degrees to those who would go no further. Count nothing for loss, but count all that has happened and is happening for gain. For the afflictions of life are in My hands. As my wings are attached to my Son who comes with healing in His wings. He flows in Me, all is of Me says your God, even my Son is of Me even from My own loins. And as He obeys me, you shall, as He perceives My goodness, you shall and even the mercies of David shall be your portion My daughter, So separate yourself unto Me in this hour as never before and the light of day shall soon break forth."

Standing in the Pain

What is pain but only a reminder of one's humanity
What is pain but a tool that teaches endurance
For God suffered the ultimate in pain
He suffered not only the pain of humanity but also the
pain of the soul
Let me Lord be able to withstand them both
With you within me.
For only with your help can I stand
You are He who gives
You are He who takes
You are He who helps those who ask
I ask Lord for your strength
For your perseverance
For your love to flow thru me
Even in the midst of the pain
You are the all giving
You are the creator of all things even the pain
You use it to teach, to reprove,
To establish endurance in me
God I will stand
I will stand and though the pain may never leave I will
stand
My love for you is more than my suffering
My desire to be like you is more than all the troubles
of my existence
I will stand in you
I will stand

11

A Case Of Deliverance

There is one particular, amazing thing that I have experienced in this walk with the Lord. This still has me in awe of the greatness of God. To try to relate all that God did and how He did it would be futile. Our minds could never comprehend the magnitude of the experience. Nevertheless, I will attempt to put down on paper the events that happened to keep a record of how great is our God.

As I left home on my way to my destination I prayed and pondered what my purpose was for this trip. Why was it so important for me to visit this cousin? We had not seen each other in many years although we had kept in touch. All the way there, I had an expectation deep in my soul but no clarity as to what, when, or where. I was tested on the way as the Lord told me to ask the woman sitting next to me about her daughter. I ignored it at first. He then said the daughter is in college. I still ignored it. However, as I continued reading the book in my hands, the author relayed a story where he had not listened and God had a message.

Luke 11:28
He replied, "Blessed rather are those who hear the word of God and obey it."

I promptly put the book down and asked the woman if she had a daughter and if she was in college. She looked at me and said, "Yes, I do but she is not a student, she is a professor." Then she asked why I had asked. I waited but heard nothing. I then said, "I don't know. God just told me to ask." She then turned her back and avoided me the rest of the trip. She obviously thought I was a bit off the noodle.

John 8:43
Why is my language not clear to you? Because you are unable to hear what I say.

I arrived to a warm welcome and my visit began. It was Saturday. As we sat, I talked to my cousin and I caught up with all the usual information so readily exchanged when two family members get together after a long absence from each other. We were invited next door for dinner. After a brief visit, we were back at Cassandra's house. All of us came in, all of us including the couple next door. We sat in what is known as the red room. Apparently it is a room, or parlor, where many conversations have taken place and much therapy conducted. It is a room that seems to take down barriers and lower peoples defenses. Many tears have been shed there and many hurts healed.

I sat and listened as the conversations began and then slowly it turned more personal and deep. Cassandra and her guests began to talk about how they have issues with intimacy, in the sense that they don't allow closeness with anyone. They have a problem trusting, even with allowing a touch, and showing emotions. They don't let anyone in. They talked and I listened. I noticed how Cassandra truly was uncomfortable with intimacy of any kind, even just talking about it. So I purposed I would work on that with her this weekend. I had thought that maybe this was what the trip was all about.

Sunday came and we had a nice day visiting St. Augustine and just talking. I noticed she was becoming relaxed and allowing me to touch her more. I also noticed that my mere presence was causing her kids to be calm. She had been having problems especially with her oldest adopted (special needs) daughter. She was 17 and had been having episodes of anger and rage that were becoming hard to handle. She had told me about it before I arrived so I was aware of it. She had been concerned about how her daughter would behave while I was there. Well, it was amazing to watch. As my stay progressed she became relaxed and did not once have any problems. She became loving, very friendly and helpful, which was totally out of character for her.

Monday we did some shopping, and I did some studying while Cassandra conducted business from home. I knew there was more to come but I didn't know what. I knew this because I was unable to sleep and my back was progressively hurting as time went on. I knew something was about to happen but it wasn't time. I had wondered, "when God?". It was all I could ask.

2 Samuel 15:28
See, I will wait at the fords of the wilderness until word comes from you to inform me.

That evening, on Monday, it was just her and I in the red room. She began sharing her journals as I did mine. It was a pleasant time. I could tell however she was avoiding deeper things so I initiated the conversation. She then began to open up and tell me things she had done, things she regretted doing, and how she felt trapped. She slowly put her walls down and let me in. I didn't say much. I just let her talk. The Holy Spirit was in the room. I could feel Him all over. She then began to cry and I just held her as tears that had been held back for so long broke the dam in her heart. She cried and I silently prayed and realized that something greater was stirring. There was a squatter on her land. She was saved but never had a deliverance. I didn't know if she had ever renounced all things from her past or if she had ever been cleansed from them. I knew then this was only the beginning. There was a battle lurking. I just didn't know how it would be accomplished.

The kids were in and out and the phone was constantly ringing. There was really no quiet time where something like that could occur. Ministry would be interrupted and therefore would not be accomplished so I prayed, and prayed, and prayed, and waited. Tuesday was a possibility. Maybe then. That didn't happen. The neighbor came over and stayed till 9. It was too late to start anything, especially when she had to get up early. She was actually relieved that nothing was going to happen. She knew something was stirring but did not understand.

I lay there in the bed Tuesday night tossing and turning. I told God "We have one more day. If it doesn't happen then it will have to wait till she comes to me in Georgi. in September. I asked, "Is that when God? Is this just getting her ready?"It was a very long nigh, and the pain in my back was so bad it was taking my breath.

Wednesday morning I felt anticipation and when I looked at her during breakfast she asked, "Today is the day, isn't it?" All day we were expecting. We had a relatively quiet day. I cooked dinner early and we had eaten by 3. Then it began. She started to become nauseous. She didn't understand why. Then she asked me, "Is it really going to happen." I said, "Only God knows."

It was 3:30 p.m. The kids had decided to go to the movies with some persuasion from Cassandra. The oldest son left for work. At 4:00 p.m. the house was silent. She asked me to put color on her hair, so we went into the bathroom. As I was putting the color on her hair I let her talk and I prayed in silence. We then had to wait, so we sat in the library were she progressively got nauseous. I then told her to just go with it, not to hold back. She asked me if this was normal and I told her yes. I had seen this many times and that it would be okay. Forty minutes went by and I asked her how she wanted to take the dye off. She said she would get in the shower.

As I followed her into the bathroom she took her clothes off and didn't even notice that I was standing there. This was totally out of character. She continued to get into the shower and as she closed the door I prayed and asked the Lord to bathe her in His river. I prayed He would cleanse her with His blood and that as the water fell on her all that was not of Him had to leave. What happened next was the most amazing thing I have ever encountered. As the water began to fall on her she began to weep uncontrollably. I sat on the edge of the Roman tub that was on the other side of the bathroom. She wept and wept. Later she told me she felt as if her heart was being squeezed out of her, as if her life was passing before her. All she ever did wrong, all those she hurt. It was all being exposed and removed. It was like viewing a movie. She then began to throw up. She would repent and ask God to forgive her. I could hear her. Every time she did, there was the sound of thunder. She said that when she would ask He would say" I have my daughter." This went on for at least 20 minutes as I sat and just softly prayed in tongues.

Sitting there I was amazed at the thunder I would hear every time she would ask forgiveness. She cried and then got on the floor and cried even more. She got up and turned off the water. I then heard God say, "It isn't finished." Then I saw a multitude of angels come into the bathroom. They were full of light. She turned back around and put the water back on. She later told me the reason she turned back was that when she shut off the water she had said to God "I can't stay in this filth any longer," meaning the throw up all over the floor. God answered her and said, "My Son stood in greater filth than this," and that is when she began to wail. Suddenly, she said she got dizzy and she heard in the spirit, "Hang on!"

She put her hands on the opposite walls of the shower with the corner directly in front of her. Her back was towards me. What I heard and saw is still resonating in my mind. She began to make sounds that would make a horror movie proud. I knew this was it. This was the demon that was being evicted and he was not happy. As I sat there and listened to it, for a fleeting instance, fear tried to grip me. "Oh no you don't," I said. Fear was gone. I wasn't scared or apprehensive. I sat straight up and I knew it couldn't leave the shower stall. There was no question. It was not going to stay in her either.

Psalm 34:4
I sought the LORD, and he answered me;
he delivered me from all my fears.

The growling and groaning got louder. It resonated all over the house. There was absolutely no way that sound was hers. No way. I then watched as her 5' 4" body got bigger. It was growing right in front of my eyes. The shower walls are 6' and her head was at its edge. She got taller as her arms reached up clawing the tile walls in front of her. Her back expanded and her skin turned red, even in the cold shower. The hot water had long been finished. She groaned and grew. For a moment I even thought she was going to crawl right up the wall. This went on for 5 or 6 long minutes. I began to loudly speak in tongues and then I commanded it, in Jesus name, to leave with the authority and power bestowed to me by the Holy Spirit. It couldn't stay and was not going to. There was no option. It was going in Jesus name. My command was short but I felt the power and the authority behind it. I was not screaming or yelling. It was direct precise and to the point.

Revelation 12:10
Then I heard a loud voice in heaven say: "Now have come the salvation and the power and the kingdom of our God, and the authority of his Christ. For the accuser of our brothers, who accuses them before our God day and night, has been hurled down.

Suddenly her arms slid down the wall and she was herself once more. As she did she began to laugh. It was Cassandra and she was laughing. How awesome is that! She laughed and turned around to get out of the shower. She then looked at me and asked me, "Have you been there all this time? What was all this? What just went on? You have some explaining to do." I told her, "Yes, I have been here and I will tell you what just happened." She dried off and wrapped a towel around herself. She came over and hugged me. Something she never was able to freely do. As she did, I prayed over her and asked the Holy Ghost to baptize her and bless her with the gift of tongues.

We sat and I explained everything that happened. I shared what I saw and heard. She told me she never would have believed it if it hadn't happened to her. When that thing manifested and began to growl, she could hear it but it was out side of her. She had no control of her body. It felt as if she had stepped aside. She could hear it and could feel it moving her arms up the wall but she couldn't stop it. I told her that it was a first for me too. I told her I was truly expecting her to crawl up the wall. She was standing on the tips of her toes not on the balls of her feet. Just like a ballet dancer, except she wasn't wearing toe shoes. I also knew that there was no danger. It was powerless to do anything. A legion of angels were there and they took him out.

I gave her some instruction on things I had seen and discerned pertaining to her and told her she now had the Holy Spirit in her and He would direct her. He would show her what to do. I encouraged her that she just has to ask and trust. She is not to go back. No compromise. It was God. He gets all the Glory. I was honored to have been there to see His mighty Hand. I never even touched her. I didn't have to, for the mere presence of God was enough. As we looked out the window, the rain stopped and there was a rainbow. God surely has great plans for Cassandra that He would care so much for her.

He lined all things perfectly. The kids were gone, the phone didn't ring and the neighbors didn't appear. God you are awesome! Thank you God, for You are good. That night she slept but was awaken at 3 a.m. by the peal of thunder so loud that it shook her bed. There was no rain or any other sound. Something broke in the heavens on her behalf.

Well, this is all I can remember. It may be a long tale. But it is a good one. Amen. God is good and worthy always.

2 Samuel 7:28
O Sovereign LORD, you are God! Your words are trustworthy, and you have promised these good things to your servant.

It Is God

As I sit and ponder
As I sit and look out the window before me.
I see the wonders of Your hand.
I see the trees swaying in the breeze only to realize
That it is You who blows and makes the wind
It is Your hand that paints the colors upon the leaves.
It is Your hand that moves the cells to
produce the fruit that we in turn may eat.
It is You God.
Your majesty and wonder goes beyond anything we
can ever imagine.
The skies blue shade was put there by You to give us
rest and peace.
The green of the grass and leaves to give us healing.
The white of the water packed clouds to wash us and
make us clean.
There is so much, so much more that we could say.
But our words would never give justice to all You are.
YOU ARE, there is nothing besides You.
Nothing will ever be or would ever be.
You are the almighty God.
May we worship You with all we are.
With all we have.
For it is all Yours.
Because from You did it all come.

12

The day my soul was mended
"This is why I call her precious"

I will write of this with the knowledge that many who read it will find it hard to believe. I will, however, never forget the truth of it and the awesome love my God has for me, His precious one.

This day was the culmination of years of struggles and wanderings in the desert. Many times I would cry out for God to send someone that would have the discernment and ability to take away my pain, my anger and resentments. No one came to my aid. I had grown into the place of accepting that this was the way it would always be.

One day I bought a book by Anna Mendez Ferrel. That day would be the beginning of what would end in the most marvelous experience I have ever experienced besides my salvation. I took the book and felt I was not to read it yet. John and Mary were to read it first and so they did. There they discovered something that we had been missing in our ministry. We were setting the captives free but we didn't know we were to mend their souls and so many still struggled and some slipped back to their previous lives. We also discovered that I had been doing something similar to what Anna does but never fulfilled the entire process. I didn't know. I read the book once the Holy Ghost released me to and I was amazed.

John and Mary began to use this method in their concealing sessions with incredible outcomes. People were changed. I was even allowed the privilege to minister to someone and it was life changing. I knew this was what I had been looking for. This was what I never had. My soul was broken and held captive. I was not whole. An appointment was made and I began to gather information. The Lord began to reveal a list of events that had caused tears in my being and had split me into pieces. These are pieces of e-mails sent during the week prior to my appointment. I have put them all together so they make sense

6/18-22/2009

I am bitter. That is why I get angry and why I have a hard time accepting others' ways of doing things. I am not happy. I never have been. I can play the part but it is just a part. I have not felt all these emotions so strong at the same time before. So many times before I have been in this place and have been passed by. All this has been brought to the surface before to just be looked over as personality traits and just ignored. Once I even begged for ministry and it was not attained. I am confused, empty, void of emotions in a way. It is as if everything is so deep inside that I don't even know where it is. I don't know how to explain it. I asked myself what would I like to be? Where would I like to go? What would I like to do? If I could do it all over again, how would I do it? I had no answer. I never remember having a "this is what I want to be when I grow up moment". I always have been tossed in the direction I thought would be the right thing. The thing that would make others happy with me. Never what I wanted, although I would not have an answer for what I wanted. I don't know to this day what I want.

I also realized that the fact that I had been a twin and that one had been lost was brought to my remembrance. My mother had been pregnant three months when she thought she had miscarried. A few weeks later she was still feeling sick and discovered that she was still pregnant. The doctor at the time told her that sometimes the uterus has too much blood and it releases the excess. It was not until I was twenty three and had surgery to remove a cyst on my ovary that I discovered that I had been a twin and that was thought to be excess blood was actually the miscarriage of that twin. This seemed to be important for some reason and the next night this happened.

I went to bed early and from 12 on I was awake every two hours. I found that strange because it was precisely two hours. Then I kept hearing words referring to two. Two, double, pair, deuce, two of a kind and so on.......

I then heard.....

" You were two and now you are one. All that was given to the other was added to you plus your own. The code was doubled."

Then it dawned on me that if there was a twin, which is what the doctor said, then all she was meant to be was genetically added to my makeup. The code was doubled. Could this be why I always feel split? Like I am two people and therefore, don't know who I am.

So rather than submit to either I have become void of any.

This is all interesting and you may ask what the point of all this is. I will begin the day of my mending. It was June 24, 2009, at approximately 1:30 PM in a small town in Georgia. This is the story.

I woke early and took a shower and dreaded the day ahead. There was a great feeling of fear, anxiety, and apprehension within me. This is common for most people that are going to participate in a counseling session of any kind, be it deliverance or healing. The difference was that they, although apprehensive, don't know what to expect and I, on the other hand, knew all the possibilities and knew that much could happen. I fought with my desires to cancel the whole thing. I heard in my mind "Why are you going to bother them? They are busy and this is going to avail nothing." I pushed through and arrived at their house. No one was home. I sat in the porch and fought with myself even more. As I sat there, I wept and felt so alone and neglected. The enemy made sure all thoughts of unworthiness and thoughts of being unimportant were on my mind. I prayed and talked to the Lord Telling Him how I missed our walks together. How I miss putting my head on His lap. I took my Bible and it fell open on Psalm 143

O LORD, hear my prayer, listen to my cry for mercy;
in your faithfulness and righteousness come to
my relief.
Do not bring your servant into judgment, for no one
living is righteous before you.
The enemy pursues me, he crushes me to the
ground;

he makes me dwell in darkness like those long
dead.
So my spirit grows faint within me; my heart within
me is dismayed.
I remember the days of long ago; I meditate on all
your works
and consider what your hands have done.
I spread out my hands to you; my soul thirsts for you
like a parched land.
Selah
Answer me quickly, O LORD; my spirit fails.
Do not hide your face from me or I will be like
those who go down to the pit.
Let the morning bring me word of your unfailing love,
for I have put my trust in you.
Show me the way I should go, for to you I lift up
my soul.
Rescue me from my enemies, O LORD, for I hide
myself in you.
Teach me to do your will, for you are my God;
may your good Spirit lead me on level ground.
For your name's sake, O LORD, preserve my life;
in your righteousness, bring me out of trouble.
In your unfailing love, silence my enemies;
destroy all my foes, for I am your servant.

My Lord what are you doing with me was the
thought I had and then He told me to read Psalm 144.
Only the first verse. This is what I am doing with you
Praise be to the LORD my Rock,
who trains my hands for war,
my fingers for battle.

This was more than my heart could bear and I broke down weeping. I felt overwhelmed with the thought of so much responsibility. I am not worthy or able. Every negative thought that anyone could think of I had thought.

John and Mary arrived home and we sat together and discussed the list of issues I had put together. John was anxious to get started. He had a vision on his way home. He had seen, in the Spirit where the major piece of my soul was being held. It had been taken there from before I was born. It was the part that was tangled with the soul of the unborn twin.

We were ready, and we went to the basement of their house for quiet and privacy. Prayer of protection was spoken and immediately an angel was with us. It was an angel seven feet tall, blue in color, holding a staff. This was unbelievable and I began shaking because I had mentioned the day before to several people that I kept feeling the presence of a staff. My dad even mentioned that he had a branch of black walnut he was going to cut and something told him not to. I told him to polish it for me, it was mine,

As the angel guided, I was sitting on the couch with Mary at my side and John was in a chair in front of me. He then began to say what he was seeing. The whirlpool was there and the angel told him that he needed to go down into the deep and take the piece from the demon guarding it. John was concerned because it was a dark dangerous place and he thought the angel would go with him. He did not hesitate however and he went in. As he descended he saw things like ghosts whirling around the vortex. Deeper he went until he was standing before the guard. He described him as an octopus- looking creature with many tentacles. One of which held my soul. I heard the demon say to him, "You can't have it. You are not taking it". I heard this myself. John replied, "The blood of Jesus is against you and you will give it up and you will do it now" .I broke down because even though I know this is real, it is even more real when it is happening to you.

He then took the piece of my soul and said, "OH! That is why the angel couldn't come down here with me. He had to stay at the top so he could pull me out". Then I heard him say several times as I felt him getting overwhelmed at what he was feeling and seeing "Take me out, take me out, take me out!"

John came over to me and took what he had in his hands, the large piece of my soul. This is the piece that is who I am. He took it and placed it on my chest. As he did, it felt like fire. I felt as if someone had put a hot bag of coals on me. I broke down and fell to the floor on my knees. John then said, "I see a wooded area like a forest. And there is a path. The other piece is there". He then said, "It is not even guarded, it was just tossed away as trash. It didn't even have enough value to guard". This piece was what was taken when I was molested as a child. My self worth, my value was tossed aside. He picked it up and put it back in me. It was hot just as the first piece. I wept.

John then says," I am for some reason jumping ahead to when you were 19 or 20. I am standing in a small back yard. It is night and there is St Augustine grass on the ground. You buried the last piece of your heart there. You buried it yourself." I immediately saw the scene as if I was taken back in time. I saw myself sitting with someone I loved dearly telling him that I could not continue with our relationship. I had to put my feelings aside and think of the logical things. I needed to think of my child and future. I needed to put my heart away. That is when I buried my heart and the last piece of any emotion. As I walked away from him, I remember feeling my heart empty. All emotions flowed out of me. Tears began to flow like never before As Ted took that piece and placed it on my chest my tears soaked his hands. He was also weeping. We were all weeping. Mary said that every time John had put a piece of my soul back, she heard the Lord say, "That is why I call her precious." This made me cry even more. I can't fathom such love for me. Me, His precious.

Then Mary said she saw a skeleton floating over me. The skeleton had a box imbedded in its rib cage and in it there were many, many little pieces. This was incredible. She didn't know. How could she? Several years prior a prophetess at a conference came to me in the audience and told me that she saw a box. I had a box and in it, there were dreams. Many dreams. At the time I felt it meant that I would interpret dreams or that I would have dreams. I was wrong. It is the box that held all my dreams. Unfulfilled wishes, things I wanted to do and be. All those desires that, through circumstances, were stolen and not allowed to become reality. The box was taken from the demon with no interference and it was put back.

John stood listening and then he said, "Your brother is here among the saints and he is giving me a blue ribbon. He wants to put it on you. This ribbon, was his mantle, and that now is yours. His mantle. That which was meant for him he is placing on you. He then came over and symbolically pinned a blue ribbon on my left shoulder. This was very painful I felt the loss of someone I didn't even know but should have. More tears,. deeper tears. Then the ultimate happened. What I would never expect. None of us would expect.

Each time as we had done these mendings for others we know it is done because there is a light that enters the room. It is the Glory that then is placed over the mended soul to seal it all back together. John stood there and said, "The light is here but...but, I have never seen this." There are a host of witnesses. They are old, ancient, They are wearing white robes. Their hair is white and their beards are long and white. They are ushering someone in." He lost it and began to weep. He said, "I have never seen Him this way. He is wearing priestly garments. His hair is white. His beard is white. He is carrying the Glory. It is big, It is a big ball." Usually so far in all the soul mendings we have been part of, the ball has been the size of a basket ball and it was delivered by an angel, not the Lord Himself. I was so undone, I could not get low enough on the ground. John was weeping, and as he was handed the ball of glory, he requested I stand up because it was so heavy he was having trouble holding it. I struggled to my feet with Mary's help. The three of us held on to each other while the Glory was deposited within me. I could hardly breathe. It was truly heavy and the experience was very humbling to know that the King of Glory Himself, dressed in his priestly garments, would see fit to do me such an honor. I have no words to express.

We ended and were, for lack of a better word, in awe of all that had just happened. We decided to go eat and then, when we returned, Mary and I sat on the porch to bask in the events. As we sat there we could not stop laughing and I realized that there was a fog all around us. This was peculiar being that there was no change in temperature or humidity. I stayed till 11 p.m. and then left to drive the hour it takes to get home. As I drove all I could do is hold my chest where the Glory covering my soul had been placed. I kept going in and out of weeping. I didn't want to lose what I had just been given. It was and is a great honor. I prayed that I would guard it and keep it always.

I arrived home and didn't get to bed for another hour. When I finally did and turned off the light I saw that the same cloud that we had seen on the porch in my room. There I laid clutching my chest and praying. I woke 6 hours later still holding my chest. The thing that is amazing is that I had not slept that long without interruption for years. I slept. When I woke, I felt different. I felt as one who had been looking through a pair of glasses that were dirty and someone else takes them, cleans them and then puts them back. You then realize that all this time you were not really seeing clearly as you thought, but you are now.

This is all that occurred that day. A day I will never forget. A day I pray everyone can experience for themselves. A day I hope to help others achieve in their own lives by the grace of God. It may seem like a story conjured up in the imagination, but I can assure you it was not. Too many things were revealed that no one knew and there were too many coincidences to be an accident. So you decide. As for me, I have, and I receive it all.

Deeper still

I go deeper still to find You,
I go deeper still to know You,
I go deeper still to see Your face.
I go deeper still, take my hand my Lord that
I may stand by You,
I go deeper still, take my heart that
it may feel Your love,
I go deeper still, take my body that it may serve.
I go deeper still, hold me in Your arms
and take me in,
I go deeper still, hold me in Your arms
and let me be,
I go deeper still, hold me in Your arms
and set me free.
I go deeper still, You are all I want
I go deeper still, You are all I seek
I go deeper still, You are all I need
I go deeper upon deeper still,
You are the lover of my soul there is no other

13

Bringing Down a Ruler
"I saw her fall as lightning"

Luke 10:18
He replied, "I saw Satan fall like lightning from heaven.

This is an account as well as I can remember of the night a ruling spirit was removed from a church's youth room. Previously from this day I was led to fast for three days. Much opposition and thoughts of others doing this job ensued. I did not argue or impose my opinion on who, what, or when it would be done. I do know what the Lord had said and it would be on Friday so I prepared even though was told they would take care of it before that.

The week came, Friday was here and it had not been done. I was not surprised. God had a plan and it was about to be fulfilled. I arrived at 5 P.M. I was met by my guard. We sat and talked for a bit and then he looked at me and asked. " Are you feeling it yet because I am not?"

We had thought the removal would take place early before all others arrived but no, not yet. So we entered the sanctuary and began to worship and I could feel the room being filled by angels and witnesses. There was a definite force manifesting and I was getting drunk in the spirit. This is a state I rarely find myself in. Some were already on the floor laid out under the Glory that was there. As others entered they also began to worship.

I had asked the Lord earlier that day who would be there and who would be participating in the eviction of this Demon. I had not received any direction so as I worshiped the Lord said, " Here I will show you Gideon's men." He instructed me to put on a particular CD and He told me to watch. As I looked I saw. Those who would be with me would be worshiping in total abandon while all the rest were reserved and poised. I knew then who would go, but not yet.

Judges 7:4
But the LORD said to Gideon, "There are still too many men. Take them down to the water, and I will thin them out for you there. If I say, 'This one shall go with you,' he shall go; but if I say, 'This one shall not go with you,' he shall not go."

I leaned over and whispered to the young lion Tom, " Are you ready for battle?" and he said yes. I then said, " When I tell you, we will go. Do as I say and this will be taken care of". Worship continued to build. Pastor was on the floor in deep thought. There were people down and people in their seats but no feeling of war as of yet.

Pastor then got up and we gathered to pray in unity as we held hands the power that began to manifest was over the top. I could barely stand. We prayed for several requests and I found myself on the floor. He then said." All this problem the root of is, the ignorance of people that refuse to see women in authority." As he prayed against that, I felt he needed to release the women of this church. He as pastor had all authority to do it and so I reached over to Mark and told him to help him do that. Suddenly I realized he had his hands on my back and was imparting a double anointing. Twice the power and authority in what the Lord has called me to do.

It was so heavy my mind left my body, and I found myself in the room with the lamp stand. There I was on the sea of glass, looking up and the flames that were burning bright. I was happy because this lamp stand is that which lights up this church in the spirit. I knelt there for a while and then suddenly was whisked off to a deep and dark place. My heart broke as I saw the hundreds, thousands, millions of lost souls. They walked around aimlessly with no expression on their faces. Their skin was ashen and their eyes darkened. They had no light in them. I was overwhelmed with grief. I could not move I could not speak but I did feel someone pouring water on my feet. They wiped my feet and then anointed them. I could feel this occurring and had an idea of who was doing it but could not seem to focus on that. There I was in this pit surrounded by these souls and asking why. The Lord said, "My heart breaks for there are so many, so many. They have no light and are so blind they can't see even a glimmer of one." I struggled to leave that place and as I was returning to my senses I felt my hands being held. On one side was pastor and on the other Mark.

My face was soaked in tears as my mind returned to the sanctuary. I began to hear the pastor still praying and releasing the women. I got up and I heard him say, " And you spirit of jealousy, you high tower!". Instantly I heard from the Lord. "Go get it!!" I grabbed Mark and told him to get Tom and Jim who were already following. I grabbed my sword and headed to the youth room where this territorial spirit was hovering. As I made my way to the door I was faced with one that was locked. I turned and said, "The door is locked we need the key!". I then faced the corner. I didn't want to be distracted by anything.

They opened the door and I entered. That is as far as my clear memory will take me. I was told that I walked to the center of the room and continued to command the demon to come down and stand before me. They then said I pointed my sword and told the demon it no longer had any authority. It was commanded to leave and go back to hell. During this time all I remember is being in the heaven-lies and as I told her to get down and stand before me, she did. She was a black figure with an etheric look, like smoke was her demeanor. Her eyes were red and her mouth was full of venom that she spews out upon those with open doors. That is why she floated over their heads. So she could vomit the poison on them as they sat in the service.

She trembled and complained. She was not happy and was defiant. "Greater is My God", I said fully knowing and trusting in Him. In the spirit, I commanded angels to come and take her away in chains never to return. There would no longer be an open door for her to enter. I watched as they came and tied her in chains and drug her away screaming. I told her she was to take her friends with her. The fruits she produced. Among them were jealousy, control, manipulation, wrath, gossip, fornication, pornography, hate and bitterness, addictions and death. I can't remember all I said but I was told I was loud and very authoritative. I remember watching in the spirit as she was drug away into the pits of hell. I was told that at the same time I was seeing this I was following the procession with the tip of the sword. When the sword touched the ground I saw her disappear into the darkness. Tom who was standing in front of me felt the ground shake.

Hebrews 11:32-34
32 And what more shall I say? I do not have time to tell about Gideon, Barak, Samson and Jephthah, about David and Samuel and the prophets, 33 who through faith conquered kingdoms, administered justice, and gained what was promised; who shut the mouths of lions, 34 quenched the fury of the flames, and escaped the edge of the sword; whose weakness was turned to strength; and who became powerful in battle and routed foreign armies.

I fell on my knees. I was very weak and my back was in pain. I had one more thing to do. Pastor earlier had told me two large pews from a funeral parlor had been donated. This, to me, was a confirmation to the spirit of death to this ministry. I knew I had to go and cleanse these pews and give them a new assignment. This was an assignment of salvation and anointing for the service of God. I was told that I got up and went toward them and began to pray and speak against any curses or attachments. I walked and moved around them with my eyes closed but seeing. I did not trip or bump into anything. After this I remember that I went to the middle of the room where I had laid the sword's sheath. I picked it up and as I put the sword back into it I said, "It is done."

As I have been told there was an anointing that fell there. A great sense of cleanliness and light had come in and the Glory was manifesting. I found myself at the back of the room hardly able to stand. I remember calling for Mark, who along with Tom ,had to almost carry me out of the room. As I was leaving I told those who had joined us that they should anoint every seat and instrument in the room for a new day had dawned.

My legs were gone. I had no strength in them. I was taken to the nearest row of seats were I laid and someone put their hands on my back. I laid there and the joy of the Lord began to enter into me and into the entire company of people there. Dancing broke out and there was a celebration. The enemy had been defeated.

Psalm 28:7
The LORD is my strength and my shield; my heart trusts in him, and he helps me. My heart leaps for joy, and with my song I praise him.

As I sat and pondered all that happened, I realized that this was my first encounter with a territorial spirit. I have been involved in many deliverances of both people and places but never a territorial demon. I have, since then, realized that when Mark washed my feet, he was washing away the old anointing and replacing it with a new one. I had been promoted. This is a very humbling place to be. I have never felt worthy or knowledgeable enough. I have learned that if you obey all He tells you to do, the when and how is always revealed. There is no need to worry or fret. I believe that if He showed me what I would come across, ahead of time, I would probably fear and not enter into the assignment. I am not saying that I never become apprehensive I do. However trusting in my Lord, the lover of my soul, the one who calls me precious, is greater than any apprehension. I do not question the how's or the when's. I obey and follow His direction. He always comes and takes care of me.

Isaiah 48:17
This is what the LORD says— your Redeemer, the Holy One of Israel: "I am the LORD your God, who teaches you what is best for you, who directs you in the way you should go.

This is all I can remember. There has since been a great manifestation of Glory and freedom in that youth room. God is good and so worthy. Praise His name forever and ever.

He calls

He calls my name and I listen.
I listen as His word penetrate my spirit like a rushing
wind
My flesh trembles as His voice commands. My heart
rejoices as I hear the voice of my redeemer calling me
to come.

He calls my name and I go
I go where he sends me I go quickly without hesita-
tion. I go willingly even unto the death of my very flesh
I go and ask not why. I go no matter where He sends.
I go for in the going I find that in reality I am following.

He calls my name and I do
I do His bidding. I do as He asks, what He asks and
when He asks. I do not wonder why for He alone
Knows. It is my love for Him that moves me and so I
do all to please Him and Him alone.

He calls my name and I come.
I come to His chamber where He waits for me. I come
expecting His full attention
There in His arms there is no other besides me. He
loves my soul, He loves my spirit, He loves me and
with His love surrounding me

I listen, and I go, to do, so I can once again come.

14

The Exposure

Romans 13:12
The night is almost gone, and the day is near There-
fore let us lay aside the deeds of darkness and put on
the armor of light.

One of my many trips to visit Cassandra. We
had decided to sit by the pool and relax which is why I
go spend time with her. She makes me relax, something that is very hard for me. Anyway we were sitting,
just enjoying the pool, when all of a sudden I became
alarmed. I had an uncontrollable need to call Mary.
There was an urgency in my spirit. I knew she would
be home since John was in the process of getting
ready for a trip.

I picked up my cell phone and called. The voice I
heard on the other side of the line was one of shock.
She did not understand how it was possible that I
would know to call her. I asked her " What is going
on? I know there is something not right".

She then had no choice but to confirm what I already knew; John was in trouble. This is not something new to me. All through the years I have known
him, from that very first night when God said you stay
with this man, I have always known when he has
struggled with something. Be it drugs, alcohol or

anger. I had been feeling an uneasiness lately but did not try to discern what it was. Well here it is.

Mary told me that he had a very rude argument with the neighbor and that it was not very Christian in the way he conducted himself. This is not the way someone in his position should act. I told her I would begin to pray and that I would talk to her later.

I got back home after a few days and began to fast and pray. I wanted to know. I needed to know. I was the watchman on this ministries wall, the armor bearer to the two of them. If there was something amiss I needed to know so I could pray and battle. I had seen the possible future of this ministry and the future God had in store for him. God had given me a glimpse of it and it was more than I could ever imagine on my own. It was beyond anything that had ever been before. It was part of the great outpouring of Gods power and Glory. The last Revival. The one that would usher the coming of the King. I had seen it and I could not just stand by and let the devil destroy such a possible future.

As my fasting became more intense things began to come to light and one by one I would inquire from Mary whether I was right or wrong. Every fear I had was as I thought. Pride had taken a deeper hold and now it had became a greater issue. The things that were the problem I will not discuss in detail only in general and as much as needed to make the story relevant. When one is placed in leadership, as he was, it makes one responsible for all he does because nothing can be below what is not above. If there is sin and corruption at the head that is what will be produced in the body. It was now affecting not only him but his family and the ministry. God was showing me this .Why? What can I do? After all he was an apostle who, many times, had said no one but another apostle could correct. How was I going to approach this? I knew he had a temper and I knew that if I said something about what I knew, Mary would be accused of having told me. She had not but that is how it would appear.

As I prayed and waited I hoped God would reveal the information I had to those he would hear from. Prophets he trusted. I went to Europe with them on a mission trip to minister for one of those men. Maybe this will be the time? No it was not. Time and time again I hoped and it did not happen. Things where escalating with him. His personality was being affected by what he was doing and Mary was at a loss

There were several horrific events during this time and as I wept and prayed during the night, asking God to show me how to help him. I would ask how I was to approach him, I would get no answer. Days and weeks went by then, in the middle of the night God woke me with the words to a letter I was to write and give to Mary. She was then to do what she felt right to do with it. Give it to him or not. My heart was on the paper and know it was up to God. Do I pass the letter on or do I hold it. I needed an answer.

That following week a conference presented itself where there would be a prophet I was knowledgeable about. He was a true man of God and I was sure I could trust any words that he would deliver. I was invited to go and decided to do so. All during the two hour ride there I prayed for God to say something.

Tell me what to do. I was desperate and was driven to get a word.

The meeting was good and those wanting a word were at the front. I was one of them. There I stood as the man of God passed me by over and over again. I stood and would not be moved. God had to speak and He did. The man came over and looked at me. I was the last one still there. He looked and then said in a loud voice, *"DON'T BACK DOWN, DON'T BACK DOWN, DON'T BACK DOWN! You are a woman who loves God, you are not to worry or care what people say about what you do, or how you do it. You are not to worry about their opinions towards you."* That was all I needed to hear. I had my answer.

Mary called in a panic a few days later. She had reached the end of her rope she could take no more. She told me she had put out a fleece. She had told God that if a certain thing happened that would be the signal to her that she was to confront him and give him my letter. It was only two days and the event occurred. The confrontation was at hand. I spent that night in prayer deeper than I have ever been before. The battle was fierce but in the end, even with the anger it produced and his unwillingness to give the issues up, he relented and did.

Isaiah 28:6
And for a spirit of judgment to him that sits in judgment, and for strength to them that turn the battle to the gate.

I was reprimanded for my assuming I could correct him. I was rebuked for knowing what I did. Mary of course got blamed for telling even though she did nothing but confirm what I already knew. He gave it up not because he wanted to but because he wanted us to shut up about it. So we did and things moved on without any further issues.

The day we were corrected for our presumptions he allowed us to do a soul mending on him. It was powerful although it was hard going at the start. Pride is such a fierce enemy of man and there was still much in him. I could see a deep part of his heart where he hides behind all this illusion. I know deep inside there is a sweet humble man. May I see it Lord.

Proverbs 29:23
A man's pride will bring him low,But a humble spirit
will obtain honor.

I am still

I did the battle
The long night of the soul
The darkness engulfed me
The pain overpowered me
I did the battle
Now I am still.

I did the battle
My heart was broken
My eyes filled with tears
My mind in turmoil
I did the battle
Now I am still

I did the battle
Now I am still
The light is coming
The pain is leaving
My heart stop bleeding
My mind is quiet
Now I am still

I did the battle
The cost yet to be determined
Outcome unknown
I did the battle
I am still

15

Encountering the Queen

Psalm 104:4
He makes the winds His messengers, Flaming fire
His ministers.

Time went by after the exposure. Time well spent on deeper things of God. All was quiet and moving towards the future. We moved the ministry to a larger place and new people were coming. They were exciting days with many angelic visitations with massages from God. Many prophetic words through angelic script and much different and miraculous things happening. Was it too good to be true?

On a Wednesday prayer meeting, an angelic script was given and many it read,*"Although you will be criticize for doing so, take authority over the Queen of Heaven and her cohorts who interfere with harmony and unity....not overlooking anything!"* At this moment I believe this was a direct mandate to me specifically. I thought that when I received it but did not come to the final conclusion until after what happened next.

When I got into the car, the following Friday, to drive to church I felt an anticipation that was familiar to me. It was not the anticipation of worship or being in the Glory although that is what I always want. It was the anticipation of a battle. As I drove there I listened to worship music and prayed in tongues so by the time I arrived I was already prepared and in a state of spiritual drunkenness.

We began to pray as always before the service. The room was hot since the heat had been put on instead of the air conditioner. We sat and prayed . Mary showed me the script again and said it needs to be done but we didn't go any further with it in conversation. The anointing was so heavy I couldn't stand and was sitting at the edge of a table until I just ended on the floor where Mary was already. I didn't care that it was dirty. I didn't care. I was so overwhelmed I couldn't even think.

Walking to the chairs for service was difficult. Worship began and it was at a higher level than it had been before. I could tell that even John was so in the anointing he was having a hard time focusing. It was great. I suddenly started feeling a pulling. This was a pulling into battle. I took my pad and wrote to Mary, "I feel pulled to a fight. Do you think I should?". I leaned over and showed it to her. She was so drunk in the spirit she couldn't read my hand writing and asked me "baffle"?. I then wrote BATTLE. She then said, "Absolutely." As soon as the words were uttered out of her mouth I was gone. I remember I began to shake as if I were being pulled out of my body by force. I was shaking so hard that my muscles were hurting. I could hear nothing but a faint sound of John worshipping. I saw a ball of fire coming toward me. This had never happened to me before. I had been taken as it were in my mind but never so physically involved. I remembered words that had been spoken by three different prophets of God who said to me that I would be suddenly snatched to do work and then brought back. Could this be what was happening?

All was dark and there was no light in front of me. I felt protected. I had no fear at all. Suddenly I felt myself land on my belly face down on the filthy dirty tile floor. Ok so I am still in the church. So where am I? Could I be in two places at once? I didn't care at all. My shaking subsided and I found myself standing in front of a great tower sort of building. There were things of the dark and demons, hanging around. There was a light coming from inside the building. I found it peculiar. You would think there would be no light in the pit, then I heard;

2 Corinthians 11:14
"And no wonder, for Satan himself masquerades as an angel of light."

So if Satan can masquerade as one so can a principality, a ruler, an authority. I entered the tower and as I entered I could see things scurrying away and hiding. They seemed fearful of me. As I walked further into the building I saw a great throne it was high and on it was this beautiful woman. She was dressed in white and she glowed in a beautiful shade of blue. Hmm, color of the prophet.

That is what she looked like from a distance. As I got closer it seemed as if I was walking through some sort of hologram I could see her image distorting the closer I got to her. Then all became clear. There before me was the image of a hideous creature. Her flesh was rotting, there were bugs crawling all over her and she had snakes all around her. The high throne was built upon thousands of dead man's bones. It was curious to see that some where totally dry and flesh less while others were still decomposing. It was as if the throne was constantly replenished by new bodies of victims.

I stood there wondering what next and then I was suddenly up close, right in her face. I said what I heard in my spirit to say. "Give it to me! Give it to me now! You have no longer any right to it!" She looked at me with much anger in her face but I was not afraid at all. She looked at me and I could see death in her eyes. She said, " I'll make you a deal." "No deals!" I said, "Give it." So I reached out and as I did I saw my hand. It was my hand but it was Jesus hand It was as if I was wearing Him. He was covering me fingers and all. I could see the scar in His hand sort of like a clear coat. Like a jelly suit I was totally engulfed in Jesus.

I reached out and again said "Give it now!" so she reached into her pocket and gave me 5 keys. They where dirty old gold skeleton keys. I was surprised but didn't say anything I thought I was here for one thing and yet she was giving 5. She then said to me, "I will give you five counties and five only." My mind instantly thought yes for now but I'll be back for more. She said, " Tell the apostle he must choose which counties he wants. Once he chooses they are his and I will have no authority there"

So I took the keys and walked away as demons were screaming at me in agony. Apparently I caused them pain. I then heard in my spirit; "So it is done for she has relinquished 5 keys, 5 counties. Take them and posses the land."

I was slowly coming back to my senses. I could feel every muscle in my body aching. I began to weep not for the pain but for the honor to do what I just did. I then heard; "For the higher you go the greater the battle but also the greater the victory. The greater it is, the weaker they are." I opened my hand to see 5 gold keys. Shiny new keys.

A week had gone by and after telling John and Mary all that had happened we had decided he would name the counties on Sunday. There was a prayer meeting scheduled so I was at their house. I gave him the 5 golden keys I had prepared for the upcoming occasion. He put them on the counter and we all went to the living room to begin the meeting.

As John began to pray I felt it coming on. It feels like you suddenly become hollow similar to when you are going under anesthesia. That is as close as I can explain the feeling. I asked for a blanket because I was cold. As soon as my knees hit the floor I was gone and back at the tower walking into the queen of heaven's court.

There she sat. I didn't hear her speak but I could hear her thoughts. She said, "He is going to proclaim." I felt puzzled because I thought we had talked about it being at the building on Sunday. Then suddenly I heard John explaining the keys to the group and I saw the queen's cohort bring a cauldron forward. In it were some scrolls. She then motioned to the demon to listen. As John began to call out counties the demon would take a scroll out of the cauldron and as he took it out it would catch on fire and totally disintegrate.

One by one this happened and then John said, "I will hold the fifth one." I was a bit concerned because it seemed I could not leave until it was done. She stood there with a grin on her face as if she had won something. Then heard Mary say we needed to get up and hold hands which did not happen for me. I was in and out but certainly not released from the tower. Then John said, after we prayed, " I believe I will call out the last county." When he did I banged on the table and said, "It is done!" and John did a sound he usually did when the spirit had released something in him. He did this sound at the same exact time. I then looked and counted 10 more scrolls in the cauldron. She pointed her finger motioning for me to leave and I did. I have a feeling I will be back.

The Warrior

The way of the warrior is a way of battle.
The path of the warrior is a road of dangers unknown.
The walk of the warrior is one of swiftness.
The life of the warrior is full of sacrifice.
The heart of the warrior is broken for others.
The mandate of the warrior is to set them free.

In the end the warrior stands never alone, although he seems to be.
For
The sight of the warriors is always towards his KING.
And those who which to walk in the path He has chosen
Must also do the same.

16

The Angel's Visit

Psalm 34:7
The angel of the LORD encamps around those
who fear him, and he delivers them.

As I awoke knowing I was being called to the shack, I was tired but knew there was something that needed to be written down. The pull was stronger than my sleepy eyes. So I was there and I was listening. There were several spirits in the room. Whether they were angels or saints or witnesses I didn't not know. There were three words that I had been hearing since waking, "the battle is fierce." They repeated over and over, and with those words I began to listen. This is what I heard; *"The battle is fierce. The flag has been taken but much warfare is ensuing for this place. The territory is of great military importance to the enemy it is a very strategic location you have taken. There is a great heavenly portal there. I know this seems incredulous to most who will hear what you are relaying, there is much most of you are unaware of. Portals are doorways or gates to time and space. He who controls the gate controls the time and space on both sides and can rule all that pertains to it. God has done this for the benefit of man. However man has given so much authority to the enemy due to lack of knowledge. It is time to claim what is rightfully yours since the beginning of earthly time. As you battle there will be many host of heaven with you. There has been several battalions assigned to you personally, as well as battalions over the three, and battalions over the corporate group. "*

As I closed my eyes I saw a multitude of angels. Some were on foot with great swords in their hands. Others I saw were on horseback with long spears that had flags on them. It looked like something out of a movie. I was having a hard time staying focused. The horses' nostrils were flaring and their hoofs were agitated. They were ready for the battle. Again I heard; *"As you see the host, you see that they are ready. You must also get ready. The territory has been relinquished by the ruler over it but you must now take it and remove those who have occupied it for so long. They will go but not without a fight and not without claiming casualties. There is a great importance for purity and right standing. Any, any, any, even the smallest sin in anyone's life who enters these battles will cause casualties. Even with all purified there can be cost. You must gather those whom you choose, and prepare. You must be in one accord. You must go into the spirit and lead the battle as one. There cannot be any fear. You must protect and cover all that pertains to you with the blood and assign guardians to them. Time is of the essence. God is on His feet and He is waiting to send Jesus. There is no time, there is no time. There is no time."*

I was feeling very dizzy and very weary. I was fighting tears. The angel who brought this message was a war angel. His name was Aliean He stepped back from me but there was more to be said. I could feel there was more to be recorded and so I waited.

Suddenly there was an old man standing behind me now. He was leaning into my ear. He was wearing a linen tunic like that of a monk. It was tied at the waist with a red sash. I heard him say,; *"The sash is weaved from the blood of innocent children. Every stitch is one drop of blood. Children, just as the child you read about, sacrificed to Baal . So have many other children, babies, that have not been heard about. Many children's blood cries have gone unheard, and so I carry it with me. Blood must be poured upon Satan's altars to keep them energized with temporary power. Because there is God DNA in every human it is infused with power. That is why purity is imperative the purer the blood the more power it carries. So Satan pours the blood of innocent children. As the battle becomes greater the more blood he needs and so you will hear of more blood being spilled in his name or by his instruction. Worry not for the children they are safe and in heaven. They went willingly to the slaughter. The battle must occur and is being accelerated. So to answer your question. The baby was sacrificed because Satan is battling in that particular territory at the moment. The principality needed to increase its power and so it needed the blood of the innocent."*

Lord why was I seeing all this. It was surreal I was having a hard time believing all of it myself. The old man departed. I felt the heat of Fire angel and his name is now clear to me. It is Fugues. He is saying; *"You will be talked about and you will be called a fool by many. Share with the few not with the masses for even in the few there will be question. They will question you, just as you also question yourself. Why is it so easy for you to hear and see while others struggle with it? It is easy for you because your imagination is yielded and open to receive. Even though you still sometimes question what you hear and see you accept it while others just erase it from their mind as frivolous thoughts. You will find that the more you allow yourself to yield and see and hear the more frequent you will and the clearer you will. Go to bed now we will all meet again soon."*

That was all it seemed I felt cool and I was suddenly tired and getting sleepy. I just realized I had been there 1 1/2 hours and it seemed like a few minutes. I went to bed. Did I sleep? No, I had so much going thru my mind every word kept resonating through me. As usual I surely questioned all of it.. If this is what God chooses then who am I to question. I have to trust in the almighty and what He is doing. I have to know that I know HE is the one in control of me and all that enters my mind. Any doubt on this could open a door to invaders and I can't allow that. So Jesus is my commander in chief, He is whom I love and honor. He is whom I trust and He is all I have.

The next day was Sunday and as I was sitting and worshiping the angel of fire came and said; *"Surround the counties you have been given. Walk around the border, encircle the enemy with prayers. Do it in Light do it in the Light. Make a map, claim and flag them"* . Then I saw a group of people driving around the border placing a flag at the heart of each county. I again heard him speak and say, *"Remember the heart is N.E from center."* What does this mean? The service ended with no unusual events however as I drove home I had an uncontrollable need to read Nehemiah 2:13-16 and so I got home and immediately took my bible and looked the scripture up. This is what it reads:

Nehemiah 2:13-16
13 And I went out by night through the Valley Gate to the Serpent Well and the Refuse Gate, and viewed the walls of Jerusalem which were broken down and its gates which were burned with fire. 14 Then I went on to the Fountain Gate and to the King's Pool, but there was no room for the animal under me to pass. 15 So I went up in the night by the valley, and viewed the wall; then I turned back and entered by the Valley Gate, and so returned. 16 And the officials did not know where I had gone or what I had done; I had not yet told the Jews, the priests, the nobles, the officials, or the others who did the work.

After reading the passage, the angel once again came and said, *"This is what it means: In the darkest hour go to the opening for passage in the enclosed barrier. The wall where external things in worship, are also at their lowest place. Move to the deep places of sin, temptation, destruction, and Satan, and the portals of useless worthless trash. Look at the boundaries of the place of peace and find they were broken down and its portals destroyed by the fire of judgment. Then continue to the place where the word of God is to flow. Then to the place where the King gives the knowledge of good and truth, to produce intelligence, where before there was none. But, there was no room for those who serve. So leave and elevate your position next to the natural realm to see the wall from a higher point of view. After surveying all you came to see, return to your point of origin and enter the portals of the low places. All the rulers of the land you survey, will not know what your task is or where you have been. You had not informed the church, the pastors, those with high standing, the government in place or anyone who would be doing the work that would be needed.*

As all this developed I found a map of the old city of Jerusalem and its gates. To my amazement it was the same shape and the five counties and the gates were in the same places as major roads. This was very weird, very detailed and very significant to be mere coincidence. And so I drew a plan and the directions on how we were to do this came on a Monday shack meeting. The following Friday night we prepared and on Saturday morning did all that had been instructed.

All seemed to go according to plan. All seemed to be as it should. But was it?

In the Night

There is a calling deep in my spirit
A calling I can no longer ignore
A calling pulling me into the night
Calling me to the fight
In the night where there is quiet of the natural
There is noise of the spirit
In the night, in the dark
The Light shines brighter
So what do you do?
You keep sleep for another time
You spend the dark time in the light
You fight in the light that shines in the dark
Sleep after all, is a thing of the flesh
In the night the battles rage
In the night the fight is fierce
In the night you are awake
So listen to the call
And come to the dark
Where the light is brightest after all
There HE is with you
There you are with HIM
So let your eyes not sleep
Let your weapons have rest
The time is short
In the night there is a calling
A calling to the spirit
Will you answer
Or will you sleep?

17

The Set Up

It was a Sunday and we were getting ready to go on a long awaited mini vacation. Mary had been wanting to get away. John was very demanding at home and she never had any time for herself so I planned a trip and we were ready. After the service we walked to the car and began to get ready. John was disturbed. He didn't want her to go. It was very obvious. He was pouting and acting like a child. It was sad to see but understandable. Mary and John, you could say, are soul mates. They are so much alike they even look alike. He depends on her for all his earthly needs and so he would be lost without her.

We finally got on the road and after a mere four hours arrived at our destination. It was wonderful and a very restful place. We were planning on doing a lot of praying and meditating. We needed some answers about the ministry and also personal matters. We would only hope that God would meet us there.

After a couple of days we were sitting in our room and had begun to pray. Suddenly we both had a vision that, at the time, seemed to be relating to one thin, but now I know the true meaning. As the vision unfolded, I stood looking at the sight I saw and heard a great wall of water it was like the water that flows over Niagara Falls. The sound I was hearing was equally defining and it was very powerful. The water was coming with extreme force and could easily take everything that would stand in its way BUT......... there stood a great door. It was at least three stories high. It was very old like those you would see in old cathedrals. Dark wood very ornately carved. This door was holding the waters back all I could see was the door no walls it seemed the walls were invisible. The door had a lock and as I looked I saw a small box. In this box was the key. It was a very small key for such a large door. As I stood there I felt my feet getting wet and there was water seeping under the door. I knew the box contained the key and it was John who could open that door.

I saw the hooves of horses, white horses waiting to be let loose. I discerned that they were waiting for the door to be opened so the water can run and wash all things away and then they can be let loose to do what they are sent to do and bring what they are to bring. Mary asked me what color the horses were after I had told her I had seen horses. She had seen the bust of a white horse like a chess piece.

We continued to pray and Mary saw the chess piece being held by a great hand. I told her that it was the knight and it was the only one that could move in a one, two, three fashion in an L shape and that is when she realized that it meant one, two, three, check mate. We had check mated the devil? It will not be accomplished that which he had intended? That is what I thought. I was wrong.

A couple more days passed and we left to go home. I took Mary home where John waited. He was unshaven and looked like he had not slept the entire time we were gone. I wondered if this had been a final battle against the thing that holds him? That pride and insecurity that drives him to a possessiveness and control. All I could do was hope that our prayers for him while we were gone had produced good fruit.

A few weeks later It all began with a bang that I would have never foreseen. I arrived as usual early but this time John and Mary were there. WE waited for the rest of the members to do the set up of the sanctuary. We had to do it every week since we only rented the building for the week ends. So we loaded into the van and then went to the street corner. The corner the Prophet had spoken of during his visit. He had said or the Lord had said, that there had been sacrifice in satanic witchcraft performed in a corner building made of bricks. There would be cell phone store across the street and the address would be close to 19--- It would also be to the left at the next light from the building. There it was. The building. I have always felt weird about that place. That confirmed my suspicions.

We drove over and took an iron spike I had been directed to take and communion elements. We parked the car got out and proceeded to the gate. It was as close as we could get. John hammered the spike while Mary proclaimed and then I poured the host and the wine upon the ground. We did this to redeem all that had gone on there and reverse the curse upon the land.

Leaving the corner we went back to the church and began to pray and worship. Mary began to tell me about how John was frustrated because Jesus has yet to visit and how he is tired of preaching and since she had a word she would be the one preaching this night. I suddenly got exasperated and said, in what was perceived as an aggressive manner, "we will meet this Wednesday..We will talk about this." Mary immediately jumped on the defensive and I promptly got a tongue lashing. I had seen her do this to others but she had never attacked me like this before. I sat and pondered and wept. I never intended to be in error

Service began and she had a very good word. It was of course about purity and holiness and a sinless life. She had a word for the woman who stands at the door. She told her that she was the gate keeper in the church and that she was to anoint all the doors every time she came to service. She was to anoint and pray none would be allowed that had any evil intent. It was good since she was definitely already working in the position of a door keeper.

Then she called me up and said."*The Lord has something for you. You ain't seen nothing yet I hear the Lord saying you ain't seen nothing yet For you are walking in today, today says the King of Kings You are walking into the days my daughter of Zion. Where all it will take is the point of the finger and the glance of the eye. You are walking into days, says the Spirit of God, that when you walk into a room demons will flee at your presence. For you are no longer a safe woman. Why so powerful says God? Because you carry.*" With those last words I was on the floor trembling. I was confused. If I am all they say I am then why all the correction? Why do they question all I see and do? I was very confused that night.

Saturday came and went with not much to talk about. I made some flags to wave since I had been led to do it the past few weeks and had not. I made three blue and purple ones and one red. Sunday came and I got to church early, as always, and I began to pray. When others arrived we put some worship music on and began to praise and use the flags. Irma and Sally arrived and had their flags. This was peculiar because they had not brought her flags in recent weeks and for them both to bring them this day was weird? Or should I say God led.

So we worshiped and war-fared, and prayed. I watched as the gate keeper, walked around and anointed all the doors. The atmosphere was changing and we were being lifted higher and then. I felt like a bucket of water hit me and as I looked I saw a woman waving black flags. I was very disturbed by this. In my personal experience and in all my studies on this side and the other, I know for a fact, that black is not good. It signifies death, mourning, lack etc and a number of other things like that. I was very disturbed. So when the praising was over I went over and told her she should not use black. Of course I knew she would tell me that it means righteous judgment. I knew she had been to that seminar where they taught that. I just knew it. It was a false teaching that was going around a few years ago that hooked a lot of people. Here I was in the face of yet another issue.

Well, she tried to explain and I tried to explain but neither was clear. I just told her to let me know next time she was going to do it. I left her and went to the prayer room and I told Mary that I had put my foot in my mouth and that I had told the lady not to wave that flag. That was the beginning of yet another beating. She said that the lady was right in doing what she did that she had a word from the Lord to do it. I said I didn't know about that. Then she said she would talk to her and I said "No! I will take care of it, since I was the one that made the so called mistake". That just made it worst.

Needless to say I didn't get a chance because Mary was going to do it. I was being treated like a child that the parent has to go fix a problem they caused. I saw her get up and talk to the woman during worship and I didn't say anything. When worship was over Mary had a word for several women and then she called the lady up and appointed her the children's gate. I didn't see that, but if God said it then that is what she is. She then told the gate keeper that she not only would anoint the door but she would anoint the gates, meaning those called to be gates. I thought that was cool.

John preached and the service was over, but not finished. After the service we had an incident with a young man who had been coming. Mary had a very strong word that included a time limit on what appeared to be his life. He questioned this and demanded she remove the word which of course she didn't. This, I had begun to question. I didn't agree with that kind of word from God. I questioned if it really was God. This had been one in a growing number of such messages. Some had been told to leave the service and were embarrassed in front of the congregation. The God I know, yes reprimands and corrects, but in love not in fear and speaking death over you. I would soon be in a place to dig deeper into this. This man had been asking for deliverance and none was given. I could not since the leadership had not allowed it. I felt so sorry and helpless to do anything for him.

This was the beginning of the end. Several more powerful words were spoken over me by other men of God while at their churches with John and Mary but I also was being constantly reprimanded. I was being reprimanded because for the first time I would not relent and back down from the fact that the flags were wrong. I apologized about the way I handled it but I would not and will never admit to black being good. Well this earned me a manila envelope with what seemed like a book inside. Mary told me to hold off on reading it. I said I would and remembered the previous week, the prophet that had visited the church, after prophesying over me and told me I was a prayer warrior and that I would travel in the spirit also said that "The Lord wanted three days from me and that He was going to show me something." Well was this coincidence? I waited the three days and then read the book in the envelope. A book filled with all the things they felt were wrong with me. I called and questioned their assessment. It didn't help they demanded a meeting. And so I made the appointment.

Fear gripped me the days prior to the meeting. A fear of being rejected and cast aside. A fear of being removed, of being thrown away with no longer any use. I began to accept all they were saying about me. I began to doubt myself and I began to lose myself in a sea of self regrets, doubts, fears, insecurities and rejections. I wrote many letters apologizing and trying

to make things right. I would do anything to be accepted I would agree with anything they said about
me so that they would love me again.

I arrived at the meeting and sat. The first thing
John said was, "I love you, and I want you to know
this is not pay back for your correcting me even
though I still do not agree with you on it." I thought
that was strange. I was not even thinking about that. I
thought that was in the past and dealt with. I guess
not. In my spirit I had a check. It felt like a warning, If
he still doesn't agree with what we asked him to do
then he is just waiting for the opportunity to start
again? It was strange.

Mary came in and sat and then I was told of all
the horrible things I had done during the seven years I
had been with them in ministry. They told me I was
the cause of many people leaving the ministry. I questioned them as to why they waited until now to tell me
this. I never got an answer, not really. I asked them to
tell me who left so I could talk to them and see what I
had done. they would not say who. so i asked to be
allowed to apologize to the congregation. They also
said no cause. That would only make me a martyr in
their eyes and they would only feel sorry for me. They
repeatedly told me they loved me and appreciated me
and didn't want to lose me but then they read their list
of the new rules for me. The three are no more. We
are not the same or in one accord. I will sit - no praying for people, deliverances soul mending, etc. unless
requested by them. No more prayer leader. No telling
people how or what in prayer or flags or anything. I
can't even make flyers. No shack or counseling. I can
still pray with the group but that is all. No more

Wednesday's with them on the porch. No more being a personal friend to Mary. He said he wanted his life and his wife back. This did not make sense.

This was devastating to me. I was hurt but I agreed to follow all they required. I was desperate to comply so not to be cast aside and rejected. The spirit of fear had a hold on me and I was in turmoil. What would I do? Where would I go? I would have nothing. They were my family. They were my life. I had committed myself unto the end with them and know I was in the midst of losing it all because of what I was believing was wrong with me. It was all my fault and I had to submit.

The following week was very hard. I felt out of place I felt alone, rejected, and worthless. I continued to go to the services. There I sat., I said nothing and did nothing. During this week we were invited to the prophets church. The one who told me God wanted three days. He invited us to a spiritual war-fare conference. I figured "why not"?. So I made plans to go. I didn't go with John and Mary as I would have. I was no longer part of the three.

I drove with a friend and met them there. As we began the service the prophet said that he was teaching and that there would not be any prophetic words during this time. Well the teaching was good but nothing new to me. Came back the next day and then the third day. There I was on the first row with a friend. John and Mary were sitting at the other end of the row. He taught and then when it was over we began to pray and close the service. As I stood there worshiping and receiving from the corporate blessing and anointing being sent forth from the man of God. He suddenly was in front of me. Even though he had said he would not be prophesying there he was. I was shaking without control. He then said...

"**As for you intercessor.**

He brings you up. He comes and snatches you away to the higher place.

May it be unto her Lord (tongues) Lord I thank you God

For yes I have said unto you my daughter

For even I've said unto you those that bless you will be blessed , and those that curse you will be cursed.

For yes my daughter I say to you this day.

Even those that you bless with your mouth are blessed and those you curse are cursed. For yes you have searched my heart and you have known my heart.

For yes my heart I've made known and reveal to you.

For you I set you as a post as a pillar in my house

Now Oh mother of zion, Oh mother in Israel get back to those things that I've caused you to be pregnant with.

Bring to birth those things that I've revealed to you in dreams

Bring into existence those things that I've re-vealed to you even in private session

For yes I need three days to share some things with you

I need the three days to make some things known to you the things of the day that is at hand

For I say to you my daughter work the land now, work the street,

For even as I said to Joshua every place were you step I give it unto you.
So now go work the city sow the Spirit of the Most high".

Doesn't he know I'm not allowed? Doesn't he see how awful I am.? How can this be? He must be wrong. How blind could I be to think that John and Mary were right. What followed was something I will carry in my soul forever.

My Soul

There is such a deep pain in my soul
Is it the loneliness I feel?
When you value more than being valued by those around you.
There is a deep pain in my soul
Is it the sorrow I feel?
When you give more than are given to those who say they love you.
There is a deep pain in my soul
Is it the disappointment I feel?
When you are always there for others but they are not there for you.
What is this pain.
Is it that I don't truly know who I am?
Is the reality in me truly that I am alone?
Who am I to listen to?

The Lord speaks and I listen to only have the seed
taken away
by those whom you trust.
Who am I to listen to?
When the fruit you have is mistaken by others as ar-
rogance and pride.
Who am I to listen to?
Who?
My soul is in a state of confusion
My soul is in a state of being tossed from one opinion
to another.
My soul is in need of peace.

18

The Confrontation

During the following weeks after my demotion many things began to happen. I did as I was told only spoke when spoken to. That, of course; was taken as me being rude. It seemed as if I could do nothing right or good enough to please them.   During the service a woman who we had been helping was confronted and accused of terrible things and then was told to get up and leave. This left the girl that was living with her without a place to stay. Do I offer? I was supposed to not do anything and yet no one was opening their home to this girl. Even Mary, who was the one to tell her she had to leave where she was, did not offer. She said that John likes his privacy. Where was God in all this? They have a huge house where was God?

After the service, if no one stepped up, I had to. I could not stand this girl having no place to sleep. I had to do what my heart was telling me to do and to my amazement it was ok with Mary. I guess as long as I could serve their purpose it was ok? In the end I didn't have to rescue the girl. She had gone to live with her family in another state and that was good.

Things were very tense and e-mails between me and Mary were a constant wave of correction. I accepted it all for fear of rejection. By now I was out of town on family business for the week and the emails became more intense. She did not agree with my helping my family. In her opinion this was enabling them to continue to use me. I didn't see it that way but again would agree. Mary then told me to read a book on the Jezebel spirit. I told her I had many times and she then said I needed to apply it to myself. Well I did.

During my reading of the book on Jezebel. I found that I could have many of those traits. I was not even thinking that this fits everyone in one way or another. I was focused on the fact that now they were saying I was a Jezebel I emailed Mary and told her if they believed that I was operating with a spirit of Jezebel then I needed deliverance. I was confused and didn't even trust my own thoughts at this point. She responded in a way that cut deep. She said they could not help me but would pray about it and would let me know.

Three days of total silence ensued. I had no mail or any communication with Mary at all. This was very painful because Mary and I had communicated at least once every day for the past seven years. We had laughed and cried together. I had been there during all her troubles with John and she had been with me during some of my troubles. Why was this happening? I was at a loss. On Friday I sent an e-mail to tell them that I would not be at church as planned. I was not able to leave at that time. They both e-mailed and asked if I could be at the church at 9 AM on Sunday, an hour earlier than usual. I responded that I would. I was excited. I thought they were going to pray for me and we were going to deal with this once and for all. I was wrong.

I left for church at the required time It was the Sunday before Thanksgiving. As I sat in the car I heard in my spirit,"Do not say a word! Not a word. Stick your tongue to the roof of your mouth". I found this directive peculiar being I was expecting to be prayed for and that requires participation but I decided God had a plan and I would obey. I will keep my mouth shut.

I came in and sat in my usual chair. I noticed there were two other couples there. I thought to myself that maybe they were there to add prayer support. All was quiet and I was not saying a word as instructed. Then John came over and handed me a letter. He then said, " You are no longer welcome here." I was in shock. I could not think. I started to grab my keys to leave when he said, " No! Stay I want to tell you what is in the letter personally." He then proceeded to tell me that my assignment was over and they had passed the test and I had not. They had been promoted and I had been demoted and so we were finished, completed, over, done, fini. He didn't know where I would go but suggested I stay in my shack alone five or ten years because I was no good to anyone. He could not trust anyone that had strived to divide his house and ministry. I had been discovered and his eyes were now open to see clearly who I truly was. Those were his exact words

I sat there in disbelief. Tears streaming down my face I could not understand where all this was coming from. I had never done any of the things he was accusing me of. Again I was going to get up after John finished speaking but he asked Mary, who was sitting next to him, if she had something to say?. She said, "It's coming". Then she bent over as she does and began to speak "the word of the Lord"...? She said, as best as I could remember, and was able to write down when I got to the car,"You, as your own physical house (referring to my home) is divided, so are you.

You have brought defilement into this house of worship. You are bipolar. You are a witch, bipolar, lesbian, warlock, full of corruption. When the warlock husband raped you in the spirit, he became one with you and so you became a house divided and a divided house will fall. You have brought cursing and defilement. You are a witch, bipolar, lesbian, warlock and you are now in the hands of an angry God. There is but a spark left in you that He can call precious. If you do not repent and get before God it will be your end. You are to go to no man or woman for help you are alone. Your days are numbered. I have not revealed the number of your days to my prophet (speaking of Mary) but it is unto death. That was the last word she said and so I got up and left. I spoke no words as I had been told by the Holy Spirit.He told me to keep my mouth shut and say nothing.

My drive home was difficult I was in so much pain I thought I was going to die. All I could think of was what I was going to do now. What was I going to say? John had made himself a spiritual father to my son. All this was going to affect more than just me. What was I going to tell my friends? I was in shock and pulled off the highway and called Sue. She immediately said she was coming to meet me. I then called Cassandra who ministered to me and calmed me down enough for me to drive home. I had to keep composure. I didn't want to show my hurt. I didn't want my husband to see yet another church of so called Christians hurting his wife. I had my granddaughters at the house. I could not fall apart. So when I arrived I just said I was no longer going to that church. There was a difference of opinion and I left it like that.

A few hours passed and Sue arrived. We went to the shack and I broke down. She talked with me and we got some things resolved between us that had been festering and then we prayed. She could not believe what had been said and she, being who she is, emailed them to confirm all. Mary e-mailed her back a few days later and repeated all that had been said. Sue was still in disbelief. "Where is the God of Mercy and love?"

Evening came and not fast enough. I wanted to lie in my bed and weep. The end has come. All I have done, prayed, fasted, pleaded, envisioned for, was it all for nothing? I will probably never know. I was totally broken but I was not out. It had and will take me time but I will stand yet again. And so the day had come and I was cast aside. While I was laying on my bed crying asking God to show me something I opened my bible and it opened to Ezekiel 3:17 -27 this is what I read:

16 At the end of seven days the word of the LORD came to me: 17 "Son of man, I have made you a watchman for the people of Israel; so hear the word I speak and give them warning from me. 18 When I say to a wicked person, 'You will surely die,' and you do not warn them or speak out to dissuade them from their evil ways in order to save their life, that wicked person will die for[b] their sin, and I will hold you accountable for their blood. 19 But if you do warn the wicked person and they do not turn from their wickedness or from their evil ways, they will die for their sin;

but you will have saved yourself. ^{20} *"Again, when a righteous person turns from their righteousness and does evil, and I put a stumbling block before them, they will die. Since you did not warn them, they will die for their sin. The righteous things that person did will not be remembered, and I will hold you account-able for their blood.* ^{21} *But if you do warn the righteous person not to sin and they do not sin, they will surely live because they took warning, and you will have saved yourself."* ^{22} *The hand of the LORD was on me there, and he said to me, "Get up and go out to the plain, and there I will speak to you."* ^{23} *So I got up and went out to the plain. And the glory of the LORD was standing there, like the glory I had seen by the Kebar River, and I fell face down.*

I said,;" Yes Lord I know this. I know that this was the job you gave me but I have failed you." He then told me to read the rest and when I did this is what it said.

^{24} *Then the Spirit came into me and raised me to my feet. He spoke to me and said: "Go, shut yourself in-side your house.* ^{25} *And you, son of man, they will tie with ropes; you will be bound so that you cannot go out among the people.* ^{26} *I will make your tongue stick to the roof of your mouth so that you will be silent and unable to rebuke them, for they are a rebellious peo-ple.* ^{27} *But when I speak to you, I will open your mouth and you shall say to them, 'This is what the Sovereign LORD says.' Whoever will listen let them listen, and whoever will refuse let them refuse; for they are a re-bellious people.*

This was very clear to me it gave me some peace. It was too precise to be coincidence. They did tie me and they did put me aside, away from all in the church. God did tell me to keep my mouth shut and I had, but I still was in pain. The next morning I got in the car to go shopping. As I turned on the radio, which is something I never do, a song was playing with words that touched me deep in my soul. God, again, was speaking to me because as I listened one verse that said,"Before you ever took a breath. Long before the world began,Of all the wonders He possessed There was one more precious." That is what God called me during my soul mending. God calls me Precious.

And so I found solace in this but it was not over. Letters were sent slandering and lying, letters to those who I treasured as my friends. It would be up to them to decide what they believed or not believed. It would be my only advice to them; "Get in the word. Check the fruit, check the love."

And so the pain increased. When I thought it was over it only got worst. From the pulpit insinuations were spoken. No name had been mentioned. Only those whom were there during the inquisition and those whom had received the letters strongly suggesting they no longer have anything to do with me knew whom they where talking about. However my absence was all that was needed for others to know who the statements were referring to.

On Sunday the 5 of December the lies and slander went beyond all comprehension. I was out of town at the time. One of those whom looked to me as a spiritual mom emailed me and forwarded what had been spoken from the pulpit on that day. The slander was grievous. Not only the lies but the fact that my name was now specifically mentioned.

Mary said that they and the ministry have been under the control of a "high level Jezebel Witch." She said God told them that He blinded all parties including me and the congregation for seven years so that they would pass the test. She said that during those seven years I had been under God's mercy and now that the blinders were off and I had been "found out" for the witch that I was.I would now receive judgment or redemption from God. I had been the cause for almost everyone in the congregation leaving, and now that the 7 years is up the ministry can start to rebuild.

Then John took the pulpit and stated that such a high level witch can also be a warlock! A witch is given 7 years to complete their assignment and if it is not completed they are demoted and sent somewhere else to start over on a lower level to earn their high level back. In the process they divide, cloud judgment, bring division, divorce, death. They are like the cling-ons when you meet them they are cloaked. They don't reveal themselves until they use and demonstrate their power on you then their cloak is down and they are exposed. He explained only high level witches can transport like I seemed to do. He misquoted things I had said in previous meetings. I was totally slandered.

His version of telling me to leave the church was unbelievable He said, I was sitting there with my leg swinging and not saying a word! Then he said to me, "I have exposed who you are. I know what you are and I want you to leave and NEVER come back. You are not welcome here. He explained by me not saying a word I admitted to what I was being called and by not defending myself or acting shocked I admitted he was right. That he stood and watched me leave to see if I had any remorse or reaction - and then he said, "See, I was right".

My heart was broken. I was in despair, alone and began to believe the possibility they were right.

No More

Lord I give up
I give up all that I am
I give up all that I was
I give up all that I ever will be
I give up

I have no more to give
I have no more to say
I have no more to do
I have no more

I leave it with you
I can no longer think
I can no longer even pray.
I have only the strength to stay
Stay at your feet.

I will sit in the silence
While the storm rages on.

My face to the ground
I can see no more.
I can see no more.

There will I stay surrounded by you
Surrounded with peace.
There is no pain
There is no more
There will I stay.

The Breaking of a Heart

It has been a couple of weeks since the year began. It has been hard so far to start a year with all that happened. I am very confused and afraid in many levels. I don't know if I am being attacked or if I am the attacker. Have I been so good at camouflaging my true emotions that I don't even know who I am? It is a question that is haunting me and causing me torment. This cannot be of God.

I may have spoken but nothing I have ever said was a lie. John was on steroids and Mary did tell me all things confirming that which I already knew. He was arrogant and prideful although deep in his heart I felt there was humility. Mary is controlling, in her house, with her children and with all around her. If they don't agree with others then they are wrong. If you can provide a solution for a need or desire, then you are ok and welcomed. They have dangerously placed themselves in a place of power and authority believing they are all knowing. That is not good.

Being with people lately is like walking on eggs. Never knowing what to say, how to say it, whether to do or not. Never feeling free to be who I am. Always feeling I have to be a certain way to be accepted. I won't do it anymore. I can't do it anymore.

I went to a service with one of my friends on a Sunday and met some people I knew. It was good to be welcomed or so I thought. It seems all things in my life are never as they seem when they start. The service was good and I felt at ease. I decided to plan visiting again the following week and see how it goes.

I guess the slander still was not over. Wednesday I had a letter from the pastor of the church I had visited and this is what was written

I understand that what I am about to say could be perceived in a thousand ways so I hope you can see my heart. When I heard through my father in law (who is a friend of mine) what happened between you and John I gave John a call to find out what happened from his viewpoint. After speaking with him I called my spiritual advisor and the leader of the church giving oversight to my church (who happens to be a friend of John's). Through prayer and the counsel of several of my closest spiritual mentors it seems that my church is not a fitting church setting for you to receive restoration in. I know you have not asked for us to assume that position in your life but wherever you attend should assume that responsibility. I will speak to John and see if he will reconsider working with you again. With our church being new, we simply don't have the time or trained team of individuals that could help manage this situation. I hope you can understand that it is not my lack of desire to see you supported but my desire to protect my church as a newborn that would cause me to discourage you from coming here. I will contact John in the next week and see if he is willing to walk with you again. If not, I believe that He should give you instruction on what the next step is in your life with God.
PS. My father in law has nothing but positive things to say about you and your ministry (He is not involved in this). My reasoning for taking this stance has nothing to do with the accusations of homosexuality or witch-

craft (warlock). I am simply processing what can be established with multiple parties and Johns statement that you had admitted to being under a Jezebel Spirit. I am sincerely praying for you.
To this I replied;

I understand your concern but I would like you to rest assured that I had, or have, no intention of being part of your church. I also want to tell you that after all that was said to me in person and about me from the pulpit after I was gone, there is no possibility that I would submit again to John's church. I have forgiven them for the things they said and hold no anger towards them at all. It is over and done. I wish them all the best and bless them in all they do and will be doing. I, however, have been released from them and will not renew any contact with them. I will say no more and I will not defend myself. The Holy Spirit told me not to. Even the day I was dismissed, as I drove there to the meeting and prayed, God said very clearly to me "Keep your mouth shut and say nothing" I obeyed and did not. I even had to bite my lip. I will not defend myself. My Jesus will and all truth will come to light some day. Be blessed and prosper in all the mighty things God has for you. You are a blessing to the earth.
Always, His Precious.
I have had no further contact with them I pray all is being blessed.

Psalm 69:20
Scorn has broken my heart and has left me helpless; I looked for sympathy, but there was none, for comforters, but I found none.

Saturday I decided to check out John's church website and just see if they had posted any new teachings where I may be mentioned. Well, there it was. A teaching by Mary on the Jezebel spirit. Lord, although she didn't mention me by name she did mention their recent confrontation with the Jezebel that was among them. So of course all there knew who she was talking about. I even heard snickering in the background as they gloated in pride over their so called victory.

Matthew 10:36
A man's enemies will be the members of his own
house (referring to the church body)

By Sunday morning I was a wreck in deep depression. I sat and decided to watch the service of the church where Sue goes. As I watched they announced that they were going to honor my spiritual son and make him an elder to the church. He told me they were and invited me but I declined and since they postponed it I had not thought about it again. I decided to go because it meant so much to him to have his mama there. I called Sue and she said, "You come and get some healing."

So I took a shower got dressed and started the 1 hour drive. On the way Sue and I hatched a few things out and had a good talk. All was well with us and we are better than before, thank God. I told her what had happened with the pastor and she told me exactly what she had asked Mary in the email those weeks ago. She wanted to know what Mary meant when she said I was a lesbian. I asked what she said Then she said that Mary had come to that conclusion through observation. I said ,"What Observation?" Sue replied "I don't know, but that is what she said, and then proceeded to go through all the stuff that she had said to you about all the things wrong with you. I only wanted to know because if she was insinuating that you and me... "Well then my dog was going to get into that fight." Sue is a woman who doesn't mix words......

I arrived at the church and parked since there was no one there. Pastor pulled up next to my car, got out and walked into the church. I don't think he recognized me. My hair was white and he has never seen it like that.

The worship was awesome and just for me. I was on the front row next to Sue. There was a song that has a line that says " Shine your light and let the whole world see for the Glory of the risen King." When they sang that it was as if I was ripped open from top to bottom like a fish. My arms were out and I saw light bursting out from me. It was like God ripped me and stood me up for all to see what was in me. Like "COME LOOK THERE IS NOTHING HIDDEN ALL IS IN THE LIGHT" It was an encounter. and I was done and undone.

Psalm 97:11
Light shines on the righteous and joy on the upright in heart.

After the word there was a call for those with broken hearts. I was the first one up there but like God always does, He leaves the best for last. My spiritual son was hugging me while I cried all over his sweater. His wife was at my back. Sue and others were all there by my side. The pastor's wife had my hand and then pastor came and grabbed my hand and it was like coming home. It was the most powerful, loving feeling. He prayed and rebuked all words curses things spoken over me. I ended on the floor. He was on the floor. I was broken, broken, broken. I have not cried that hard in a long time. I was a ball of tears on the floor on Sue's lap. Pastor's wife was sitting in front of me pouring words of encouragement. "God says! Raise up! Raise up, raise up!" Then a lady came over and had a word. She is prophetic and knew nothing of what has happened to me. She spoke, " I don't know what has happened but I hear the Lord say "Get up". You have not seen anything yet. You will teach men women even children. There is much for you to do." Then she laughed and said,; "She needs a new Holy Spirit baptism. Not for speaking in tongues because she is fluent in that but a baptism of joy and laughter."

It was so much I can't remember all that was said. All I know is when I got up from that floor I was not the same as when I went down. I came up new. I don't care what anyone says about me. I am open so the whole world can see. I had a peace and a joy I had never had. It is weird and I sure hoped and prayed it would last. My heart was being mended and now it must heal. I asked pastor as I was leaving, " So pastor can I come back?" He said I never told you to leave He hugged me and hugged me again like he didn't want to let go.

I emailed him today to see if I can talk to him and tell him all that happened and what was said. I want all out in the open. I asked my spiritual son if I should do this and he said that it was a good idea. So I am waiting for him to respond and tell me when I can go. I will bring the letters and the emails I don't want to misquote anything.

It is peculiar but every time I think of them I feel sad because they lost so much. I loved them and I was faithful to them. Some day they may see that but then again they may not. It is not for me to decide. My heart has been totally broken. My soul has been ravaged. My spirit tormented and yet I feel no fear, or anger, or resentment. No weapon that they have forged against me will prosper. Not because I send it back to them or wish them any harm. I don't. I bless them and will continue to bless them. I have no control over what God will decide to do with me or them. God wins and I am HIS.

Psalm 15
¹ LORD, who may dwell in your sacred tent? Who may live on your holy mountain?
² The one whose walk is blameless, who does what is righteous,
who speaks the truth from their heart; ³ whose tongue utters no slander,
who does no wrong to a neighbor, and casts no slur on others;
⁴ who despises a vile person but honors those who fear the LORD;
who keeps an oath even when it hurts, and does not change their mind;

5 who lends money to the poor without interest; who does not accept a bribe against the innocent. Whoever does these things will never be shaken.

In the Morning

With the sorrow of the night
Here is another day.
Does the pain ever truly go away?
Does it pass as the night or does it remain till morn-
ing?

The pain in the soul of man
So deep and raw,
So full of sorrow
So diligent in its pursuit.
The pain. Does it ever leave?

Does it just step aside for a while
As it gives its host a bit or rest
Or pretends it's not there so it
Can resurface when least expected?

And yet without the pain
What emotion would we have.
Without the pain there is no joy
If we have not the knowledge
Of pain we would not have
The joy in the morning when it finally comes

20

But God

Although I had received a great healing at the church that day I was still feeling weak. I was depressed and felt like there was no longer any purpose for me in this world. I could not stop thinking of all the things that had been spoken over me. There were so many hateful things that people heard and believed. I kept hearing, in my spirit, the voice of the enemy telling me they were truth. I was all those things. I was in a battle for my very life. Could this ever be over? Or will they get the final say and my days are truly numbered and over soon?

God always has a way to bring healing to His people. Sometimes it will come in the most unusual ways and then we must discern how far to go with it. Sometimes the healing comes from this one or that one but if we continue with one or the other it may be too long and then be harmful.

He may be a janitor and a man of lowly stature and demeanor but he is a giant in the spirit. We sat and talked for a little bit. He didn't want to know anything since God had already told him all he needed to know.

I was being oppressed and was being killed spiritually and then physically.

So after short conversation he said,; "You need to first eat protein. Your body needs to be rebuilt." He then said, "let's pray and anoint." He laid his hand on my friend who had come to join us, and anointed her and then himself. He pleaded the blood of protection. He did not anoint me because if he did it would keep that which was going to be cast away from crossing the blood line. He laid his hands on my head and began to pray. He broke all words spoken over me. He spoke to my mind to be healed and whole. He spoke my destiny back in order and then after other prayers that I can't remember, anointed my head and sealed it all. It is now my job to keep it away and not pick up the trash again.

As he was praying I saw the scene I had seen a couple nights ago in a dream. I saw myself in a pit tied and gagged and bound, fully guarded by demons. As he prayed, and I agreed, I was released and pulled out of the pit. Light flooded my soul and water flowed from my belly. My hand was up in worship to my King for there is no other in me. I was not possessed by anyone but the Holy Ghost and that is the way I plan to keep it.

As we ended I felt relief. It was hard to believe but I also knew this was just another piece of my healing. I should know that all things with God are simple and quick but also come in layers as we are able to receive them. No screaming and long trying prayers just authority and faith. I gave him a copy of my testimony. I wanted him to know who I am. This would end being a mistake. He didn't understand and as I had been told by the angel, "Share only with the few." I should have kept the testimony to myself. This man is an instrument of God and used in a very mighty way, but he is not open to the things that are happening know. That is fine and that is his calling. I have to follow what God is doing with me, and that is a very different thing. It is not the usual but the unusual. God is doing new and greater things. He is pouring out His Spirit upon all flesh. He is giving and showing the mysteries of heaven to many. I sat after the prayer and I opened my bible and I read to my ever amazed mind.

Matthew 5:10-11 (The Message)
10 "You're blessed when your commitment to God provokes persecution. The persecution drives you even deeper into God's kingdom. 11-12 "Not only that —count yourselves blessed every time people put you down or throw you out or speak lies about you to discredit me. What it means is that the truth is too close for comfort and they are uncomfortable. You can be glad when that happens—give a cheer, even!—for though they don't like it, I do! And all heaven applauds. And know that you are in good company. My prophets and witnesses have always gotten into this kind of trouble.

So I am in great company and I am blessed to be persecuted. It is a privilege for it means I am a threat to the kingdom of darkness and that makes me happy. I am serving my Lord and King.

I have realized that I had been guilty. I had not listened to the Lord. Many warnings He gave me. I chose to listen to the interpretation of others rather than to inquire the truth myself. I have been guilty of not seeking Him for answers. I was guilty of agreeing with things I knew deep in my heart I should not have. I should have listened. If I had then, I would have left before being removed. I would have avoided these things. I chose to do things in my own power. I chose not to rest and be still as He was commanding. I listened to the wrong voice even when I knew I shouldn't have. Yes I did learn much even during all this. What a way to learn. It has been a very hard lesson. Many words given to me, through dreams and angelic script, told of the coming confrontation and then slander. At first we thought it was meant for Mary since she had been so rough with her words to people. There was one discrepancy. Mary, after I was removed, said that the words were referring to me. That I had been slandering for seven years and know that I had been comforted. I was silent. This is in error. God doesn't say things are in one order and then flip them. The word was; "There would be a confrontation and then the slander." That is what occurred to me. I was the one confronted and then slandered. Several such things I have uncovered (too many to list) pointed to the events that transpired. God knows and I pray mercy on all things.

I have come to understand that God doesn't speak and anoint something that is defiled. Looking back i have seen the many times i was cast away or slandered only to find later that those who did paid a deep price. Some became ill some lost ministries and marriages. All they spoke against me fell upon them. They call that karma. If it was true that I was all that was spoken when I was executed, then God is a liar. God forbid. God doesn't fill a defiled vessel with pure water. He doesn't put opposing things in one space. It doesn't work. You either is are your not. You are either light or darkness. You can't be both. And if all they spoke about me is true then all those prophets of God were speaking falsely.   These are words spoken to me from God through several prophets. No one knew each other and I never requested the word. I always have felt if God wants to give me a word He will send whom He chooses to give it. During all these services I was never in line or looking to be seen. I usually was in the back of the room praying. This is what HE has said about me and to me. I will not mention who gave the word just the date for it is irrelevant. It was a word from God and God can use anyone, even a donkey, to give a message to someone.

Numbers 22:28

Then the Lord opened the donkey's mouth, and it said to Balaam, "What have I done to you to make you beat me these three times?"

1984. -The year I was delivered the Lord changed my gifting from the devils use to His
The gift of knowledge, sight

1994- Sometime within this year a Prophet came to preach a revival at the church I was attending. During this time I had no idea or knowledge about impartations or mantles, nevertheless. At a service, I will never forget this man of God took off his jacket and came over to me as I was praying for someone. He placed it over me. It was something remarkable to me. The weight of this jacket was more than it possibly could be in the natural. I kept this in my heart for I had no idea of it's purpose but I do now.
The mantle of a prophet

2001. - **A** pastor with prophetic gifting came to the church to do a women's teaching. Afterwards she, was to activate weapons of battle. The women lined up and one by one she took their hand and rose it up in the air as she crossed their chest from left to right. Then she was standing in front of me. She looked at me and said. "Oh my you don't have one sword you have two" One for the spirit and one for the soul You don't cross yourself with one hand but with both".
The weapons of war

2005 - "You will go through the valley to the nations, to all the people. You will be protected You are not orphan. All is in my timing. I Am till the end. There will be no trouble without a way of escape. I Am the truth, giver of life. All things come thru me. Look at Me, Look at me (Peter) I will hold you and keep you. I work from the end to the beginning There is a reformation in the church coming. I grant sleep. I call you where you have never been Your are a fire you are a candle. Messengers on assignment. One word at a time. Missionaries. You will do things only you can reach. Each one has your own destiny! Am time. Go forth in power and strength. I am sending you forth. It has been planned from the beginning. Be ready. Do not hesitate. Go to all places. Do not falter or confound. You are going through. I Am the Almighty One. I will accomplish all I have planned. I Am the healer and protector. As close as a whisper my little ones. All from different paths to this purpose. One thing at a time. One word at a time. stay on me. Write down all you dream and see. Do not hesitate when I send you. Just do as I say and ask you to do I am all power, If you acknowledge Me in all your ways. Do not look through the natural eyes look through the spiritual eye. You will have understanding you never had before."

2006 - You have been in the shadows of others. Come out and don't go back. You are a messenger, courier of the fire of God and the word of God. You have been in the throne room. Much travail. Revelatory gift to be released.
Messenger, courier of the fire of God and the word of God.

2006 -   Deborah anointing -Seer, prophet, judge
        Three shield s - Platinum, silver and brass
        So far 3 anointing, 3 shields, 2 swords

2007 - Razor-sharp tongue in your mouth, that you will speak forth things of God and the enemy will flee seven ways where it has come in one way.

2007 - *(transcribed from a recording)* Greater authority... there is a release of greater authority, greater authority. greater authority. Greater authority. For God is calling you above and not beneath. You'll rise up above the situation. "God says that you'll walk on that which you used to be part of for it is indeed under your feet. Those enemies and those things that would come and whisper and say, "but you might come back to our side, No!" says God. "For they are under your feet. I've called you to a higher position and I've called you to a higher place. I am surrounding you with an angelic host of warriors whose blades are sharp and

they're honed and they're going to the left and they're going to the right, to and fro protecting you front and back. A greater authority. The greater authority to speak. You'll speak into dominions. You will speak into principalities, you will speak over powers, and you will see these things crumble, for God say's, "I've called forth the targets, that of a mighty warrior, and indeed, such as you have, you will release and you will give forth, and as you call it forth and as you cry out come down dark thing, even the very pillars on which that principality stands will begin to crumble at the word. They (your words) will reek with power and they will cause havoc in the kingdom of darkness!," says the Lord of Hosts, Oh! Oh! Glory to God!
Great authority

2007 - *(transcribed from a recording)*For you! It is an interesting vision
I see a vision, I hear the pegs are falling into the right holes. And then what I saw was an open landscape and you were digging for fence posts.You were putting fence posts, in the landscape getting ready to erect fences.For this is what the Spirit of the Lord is saying." I Am calling you forth right now," says the Spirit of the Lord. You will be a divider of men's souls and men's hearts. You will build the fences and will say "Here is the house of the Lord, there is the house of Baal. Choose which side that you will cross, which side that you will live in. For now as I am preparing the fence post to drop in the ground, the avenue is open for you to cross over but once the fence goes across the fence post there will be no crossing." He is calling you to divide. He is calling you to conquer, He

is calling you to separate. For even the Lord Himself said " I have not come to bring peace but a sword. I will turn a daughter in law against her mother in law, son to turn against his father, even now He said in that day I wish I could release that fire". And the Lord says " Now is the day and I release that fire upon you. To separate, to distinguish, to enable, to disable. The power to release a decision. Call it forth."

That is interesting. To enable,to disable, to empower, to remove power and you are just out there digging in the fence posts, digging in the fence posts. Ability to speak the word to enable, disable empower and remove power

2007 - You have dug with your elbows your hands, shoulders, knees, feet, even with your loins. You have dug deep and you have guarded the ditches. It is time to move for others will mow guard the trenches you have dug. You have spoken and not been heard. Time is coming for a change. 6 months, 6 weeks, 6 days? Not clear Yahweh becomes one with you. You are given a triune anointing. You have stood and persisted in the shadows. you have dug in your heels. You stand and have stood alone. For the work you are assigned to do is in the heavenlies. You will speak over nations, countries, villages governments. In the heavenliness you will function alone. Apostolic anointing, you will prepare others for war. You have suffered the sufferings of Christ. When you run you run into Him for it is were you get your strength. The Lord is giving you a Sabbath rest of three days. Take it you choose when. Triune anointing.Power in three levels

2007 - *(transcribed from a recording)* "In the mighty name of Jesus Ha... I am hearing a strange word..... Strange when I laid my hands on you. SHOGUN Ha... What in the world is Shogun......In the mighty name Oh warrior....... Fill, fill, fill, a double portion, double portion, double portion, double portion, double portion, double portion, Fresh Ohhhh......Mercy favor increase, increase, increase, increase, increase, increase, more, more, more, more, more, more, more, more, more, more. In the Mighty name of Jesus increase, more, more, more, more revelation, more insight, more increase to discern the wisdom of God. In the Mighty name of Jesus bring forth those things. Favor, favor, favor, increase, increase."

   OH MY LORD!!!

Im a shogun

I later looked up the meaning of a Shogun.... A supreme military commander willing to lay down his life and who answers only to the king. WOW!

2008 - As He took my hand I felt as if I was being spun at high speed. I was getting very dizzy and overwhelmed. He then, after imparting more power and anointing more authority in the spirit. He said he saw a ring. The ring was the color of leaves or jade. "You probably know better than me what this means". There will be more authority to speak" were his words. Then he let go and I felt as if I was falling to the ground although I was already on the floor. It was weir but also a very amazing feeling. This is what I have found about this.

   Green is the color of the prophet and indicative of divine activity. Linked to wealth   and   prosperity as well as spiritual well being and prophetic operation.

The fact that it was jade. The stone jade symbolizes divine mandate.

A ring is a circle with no beginning and no end.

2009 - *(transcribed from a recording)* You will be called the three. They won't even know your name because it will be the three...... you will be one who has spiritual jerks. That is to say you will be praying and then suddenly like in a jerk you will find yourself in the persons presence. You will be there to cast out a demon. You will have angels at your disposal and you will know them by name. You will also know the names of the demons that stand before you. You will suddenly just be there and then be gone **I will have the ability to go into the spirit realm and do battle**

2009 - "DON"T BACK DOWN, DON"T BACK DOWN, DON"T BACK DOWN. You are a woman who loves God. You are not to worry or care what people say about what you do or how you do it. YOU ARE NOT TO WORRY about their opinions towards you. Then he rubbed his hands down my shoulders and said " Let there be healing in her body her entire body, No more pain". Then he put his hot hand on my head and said," You will see angels, many angels. You will not only see them, you will converse with them. An increase of the supernatural, more of the supernatural. I see chariots coming. Many chariots You will have many angels at your disposal. I can hear the hoofs on the horses as I speak. I see chariots of fire". Then his assistant (who travels with him) started blowing on my hands and head. He then said "I see chariots of fire coming to get you and WOW!, it isn't an angel driving the chariot, it is the Lord himself dressed in priestly garment. He is the one that will come to get you and take you places. The Lord himself is coming for you".

End of 2009 - He said this woman hears from God, she sits with God, she knows God. He started to rub my back right where it hurts and began to whisper to me to let go of the hurt, the pain, the resentment. He then began to prophecy over me. There would be doors opening for me, I would have a healing anointing, even unto raising the dead. I would call the dry bones to life. There are rivers of waters, fountains of waters that will bring drink to the thirsty. I sit in the throne room.

2010 - Sitting in the back of the room he came towards me and said. You will wright a book. No! Two books and they will sell in the thousands. He then left and came back and said I would be teaching many spiritual children.

2010 - I impart to you the mantle of prayer? I think I can't remember. I was so engulfed. I could feel myself falling but I was not. I could still feel them holding my hands. I was lost in the smoke. I remember I was on the ground and let go of their hands. The prophet kept speaking over me. He kept calling prayer anointing on me he then started blowing on me. I think he blew on me three times and was hitting me with the prayer shawl he was carrying. Over and over he struck me with it. I could feel shocks of energy every time he did.

I was lost in a smoke of lights. I was lost in a whirl-wind of emotions and it felt as if I was loosing myself. It was something that words can't even start to express. I screamed as I saw the lords feet in front of me I reached my hand and touched them. He was there in the smoke. .... Suddenly, the prophet turned to me and said about you. He then said.... I would be one who will pray and I will go to where I am praying. I will be like Philip in the book of Acts. I will be taken suddenly and will be in another place. I will see clearly where I am so to describe in detail. I will do this very frequently. I will do it a lot. He kept repeating that it would be a lot and very frequent I would be at a service and the feeling would come and I would say," Can I please hear the sermon", and I would be gone to some other place. CRAZY! I also believe I heard him tell me I already do this. But I am not sure if it was him who said it or me who thought it. I have done that several times but   I guess it will be a whole lot more often.

2010 - *(transcribed from a recording)* The Lord has something for you.You ain't seen nothing yet. I hear the Lord saying you ain't seen nothing yet. For you are walking in today, today says the King of Kings. You are walking into the days my daughter of Zion. Where all it will take is the point of the finger and the glance of the eye.You are walking into days, says the Spirit of God that when you walk into a room demons will flee at your presence.For you are no longer a safe woman.Why so powerful? Says God, " Because you carry."

2010 - The Mantel of St francis of Assisi was placed on me. Now I know why I have always been so attracted to him. Now I know why animals listen to my commands, why music is so important , why poetry seems so easy, why my heart is so hurt over the church why I hurt in my body and why the palms of my hands hurt. Now I know why all the words concerning God's power using me to cast demons, even with a word or a look. Now I know why I take heavenly trips. Now I know because he did all these things. May I be worthy to follow him.

2010 - *(transcribed from a recording)* "As for you intercessor.
He brings you up. He comes and snatches you away to the higher place.May it be unto her Lord. Lord I thank you God. For yes I have said unto you my daughter. For even I've said unto you those that bless you will be blessed , and those that curse you will be cursed. For yes my daughter I say to you this day. Even those that you bless with your mouth are blessed and those you curse are cursed. For yes you have searched my heart and you have known my heart. For yes my heart I've made known and reveal to you. For you I set you as a post as a pillar in my house. Now Oh mother of Zion, Oh mother in Israel get back to those things that I've caused you to be pregnant with. Bring to birth those things that I've revealed to you in dreams. Bring into existence those things that I've revealed to you even in private session. For yes I need three days to share some things with you. I need the three days to make some things known to you the things of the day that is at hand. For

I say to you my daughter work the land now. Work the street. For even as I said to Joshua every place you step I give it unto you. So now go work the city. Sow the Spirit of the Most high!

November 21, 2010 I was executed

Since then few words have been spoken over me. One said I would never be part of another group I was a nomad. That was sad. Then in February 2013 a prophet said to me, after speaking over those with me, " You are misunderstood and that is why people do you the way they do. God says He likes you just the way you are. Don't change. He likes you Sassy classy"

Recently I was told again to write the books. I was also told that because I am so close to my God the darkness fears me and is very threatened by me.

So here I am carrying all these things in my soul wondering what I will do? Where I will go? I am not a young woman anymore and don't have the strength I once had. But God is OH SO GOOD! He redeems all the enemy has taken. He redeems all things to those who truly love Him, and I do. As I was waking the other morning I was in the midst of a short dream. In it there was an angel in a robe. It had an ornate band at the bottom at the hem. The rest was white. He said to me,; "Don't give up Pearl". I didn't feel He was calling me pearl as an adjective like say-ing sweetie. I felt in my spirit He was calling me Pearl as if that was my name.

The next day a friend and I were talking. I told her about it and we both said. How do you get a pearl?" You get it through friction and pressure. A grain of sand finds its way into an oyster where it is covered with a layer of diseased secretion. The grain of sand is causing the oyster friction and so it tries to cover it. WOW I have caused friction and pressure which in turn caused much poison as a means to cover it up. But all that it did was make me more valuable.

Pearl means, 'Something of great value'. God's truth, God's people formed through suffering, to endure and a costly experience. It also means loyalty, faithfulness and friendship. Modesty, chastity and purity. Spiritual transformation, charity, honesty, wisdom and integrity, all the best within us.
God now calls me not only precious but pearl. I am "His Precious Pearl."

God has redeemed many things in my life. I have made new friends and healed relationships with old ones. My friendship with Ann, God restored and it is even stronger than it was. There is a saying that is used at weddings but it isn't exclusive to marriages. " what God puts together no man can put asunder". My friendship with Ann was put together by God and even after all that got in the way, all the lies that were told and listened to, no man could break the bond. I have one regret, that it took so long to get to this place.

Why ask?

Why should you ask for anything?
Those whom you ask will probably not reply.
Why should you ask?
Those whom you ask may not reply.
Why ask?
Those won't reply

If you ask you may be ignored
If you ask you may be rejected
If you ask you may be disappointed
If you ask you may be hurt.

Ask only of God
He is always there
Ask only of God
He will give you all things
Ask only of God
He will never hurt you.
Ask only of God.

Do I Dare

      I have not until now, been in the frame of mind to write of the events that occurred while visiting Cassandra. I have and still am questioning even though much less.

I arrived after spending the week vacationing and visiting my children. My husband dropped me off on his way home. We spent two days just relaxing but deep within me was an anxiety that I could hardly contain. My husband left on Monday and the rest well it is hard to remember the exact date of the occurrences but this is as best as I can remember.

      When I arrived Cassandra began to tell me about her issues with color and how they made her sick. She couldn't wear it or have it touch her body. Even hair color was aggravating her and so she had not done that in a while. She told me all this started after she fell hiking and injured her breast bone. I pondered all this and wondered what was going on.

      That evening I was listening to worship music while laying in bed. And began to download things. The Spirit told me her chakras where out of line. Her colors where out of tune and then began to tell me to go and buy stones for each of the Chakras. I needed to find fabric in each of the colors and this must be all natural. I must find a way to play the notes for each and then she must wear all white, all natural fibers. Lay on a white sheet surrounded by the 4 elements in their proper placement. The sound had be played in 3 minute segments, 3 times with a 1 minute pause between notes. All was very precise and detailed. I began to question what I was hearing. I asked God to please let me know if what I was hearing about, how to help Cassandra, was truly of HIM and then I turned the page of my journal and at the top of the page was written, "Your soul's emphasis is always right". My soul's emphasis has always been to help and relieve suffering, so my soul is right and it is God. Immediately I heard in the spirit. "Did I not create everything? So then, is this not mine?"

The next morning I told Cassandra and Rose, her best friend, what had happened and we left to go get what was required. We went shopping and acquired all we needed. All the things we needed we easily found. That was amazing in itself. That evening I made all the preparations and we began. Cassandra laid on the floor as instructed and Rose began to play the notes on the key board. One by one the notes colors and stones were placed. One by one the vibrations began to increase. When we finished we waited. Rose and I had soft music playing and as we sat and observed Cassandra, we saw as her body bent and shook. She moaned and shook and bent her back. It continued for at least 20 minutes. Rose was shocked to see her doing what she was doing and asked me if it was demonic. I told her I did not feel demonic I felt alignment.

As usual she relaxed and then said, "You have some explaining to do." Cassandra was tired and sore and all we could do now was wait and see if it worked. They both went home and I sat in the living room crying and wondering if I had crossed the line, but didn't God answer me? I needed to go on faith of what I was hearing from God and not what I had heard from man.

I then received some angelic script for Cassandra and for Rose which I would later translate and give to them .

"The life span of trouble is dependent on your ability to remove it from your space. Kill it quickly and it will soon fade and be forgotten."

The next day we rested and just visited. To the amazement of all, Cassandra was healed. She had color on her and no more issues with it. WOW that was awesome . I wondered if God had something for me too. This week was quickly arriving at the year mark for the events that had so painfully destroyed all of my being. I wondered if there would be healing for me ? Will I get a turn?

As evening came and I got ready to get in bed, there again was the questioning and the worry. Am I a witch. Is it true God?, was the question in my soul. I cried as I recalled Cassandra's alignment that had happened a couple of days ago. God had really done a work? Did I really hear from Him or had I truly crossed the line and become what I was called, a witch? I asked God over and over and then I heard as clear as if He had been standing in the room. "YES YOU ARE A WITCH!". I was so hurt I fell to the floor weeping. "My God, whats to become of me," was my cry. Then suddenly again I heard. "You are a witch. You are a **W**illing **I**nstrument **T**otally **C**ompletely **H**oly. I said yes Lord I will own that. I hear you forgive my doubt and unbelief. The trembling in my soul. It shakes me to the core of my being. Lord Jesus is all I can speak. I pray all is as it should be. I pray I am all I should be. I pray I do all I should do. Let me not go the wrong way.

Are all these things coincidence. Is the fact that the song that happens to be playing when walking into the room is speaking of what I need. Is it wishful thinking. Is it truly God. Oh my Father make these doubts leave. Let peace come and faith in who you want me to be raise up. Even though I heard what I heard I still had fear. I still questioned. Too many things where being spoken in my ear. Too many messages disguised as songs or signs on the side of the road. "Lord let me settle in my soul" was my cry.

During this week, during the night spirit would give me short quotes that to this day I find hard to believe I heard. These are the quotes and teachings

The limitations of man are due to the insecurities of knowledge. He trusts only his understanding and so he is limited. God has provided through His spirit a limitless well of wisdom. His wisdom is there for the asking, If a man would only open his ears to hear, his eyes to see, his heart to receive without doubt. Then all, all, all things would be possible on this earth as they are possible in the heavens. Ask and you shall receive... There is a cost. YOU must put action into it. First you ask without doubt, then when you receive you must accept without question.

Sometimes to understand something you must first remove understanding.

Leave your brain at the door. Bring only your imagination

The more complicated the question the simpler the answer

I used to write with the words of philosophers and eloquent speakers to only find that truth truly lies in the simplest of words.

A door mat lies lifeless on the floor while gathering the dirt as people walk over it. A door post holds up the roof keeping all safe inside. Be a door post

It is the nature of things to express the knowledge of the Spirit

There are places in life that are like a lovely pair of stilettos. You see them in the window of the store, you like them and so you bring them into your life. But then when you finally put them on they are tight and end up giving you blisters. Why? Maybe because it was the wrong pair of shoes. I prefer flip flops.

Thankfulness is an expression of the gratitude you feel, when you know you are all you can be, and you have done all you can do, for yourself and others, while on the place and time the Creator has given you.

Having no regrets over the things you didn't or couldn't do sets you free to do the things you can.

Never give an opinion that you are not first willing to apply to yourself.

The visions of man are most often clouded by the light intellect. If only he would turn off the switch he could then see clearly.

Like a radio you can receive messages from the Father God. Just listen, submit, and obey.

Awaken your soul to the Glory of God and see His mysteries unfold.

My visit was almost over and I still had not received my alignment. I wondered if this was for me to do but not receive. Well I was wrong. Cassandra and Rose told me after we had our nice supper that it would be their honor to align my chakras. I was excited and apprehensive all at the same time. I didn't know what to expect or what would happen to me. I have always been very hard to minister too. I guess I have too many walls.

There I was on the floor, stones in their proper place. Musical notes being played as they were instructed. There I lay and was feeling nothing but very cold. I could figure out what was going on. Cassandra came over and did some reiki and laid her hands on my heart. That was all it took. I began to weep and shake. I was getting colder and colder.I couldn't move and I felt I was not even in the room. Rose finished playing the notes and she moved around me to change the music on the I-Pod. I grabbed her leg and whispered to her to leave it. She later said I was so cold I felt like a cadaver.

This went on for it seemed a long time. I slowly began to come out of this space I was in and as I was waking into a more conscious state I heard Spirit say, "You have died. Your heart was too broken to fix so I had to give you a new one. I am giving you those 7 years back you are no longer 57 years old you are now 50." I was shaking and crying and it was hard for me to talk.

When it was all over and I was able to tell them what happened they were all amazed as I was. Rose also had the opportunity to receive. She was blessed with laughter. A laughter so deep within her belly that she said for days afterwards she was sore. It was just what she needed.

I am so often amazed at how Spirit always knows exactly what each person needs and how they need it. We are all different, God created us totally unique so why is it so hard to accept that we are to receive healing in different ways. I pray some day as those in the church box awaken that it will be more acceptable but for now I must walk very carefully and be cautious of whom I share my experiences with.

What Will Tomorrow Bring

It is very hard to end a book about ones' experiences since there is always a new page being written and a new story to be told. Through my life, I have witnessed many things and many manifestations. I have seen angels and demons alike. I have been in the glory and seen the power of God. Praise God for His mercy and grace. As I have walked with the Lord, I have gone through many battles and attacks. I have fought and won some, and have also lost some. You can deliver the freedom of God to people, but it is up to them to keep it. I have seen the casualties of religion and wrong beliefs. I have gone places no one would dare enter and have been ejected from some I had gone to help. Even through all that I have been through, I will go on. The love I have for God is greater than any problem I can experience during my short time on this earth.

If only the heart of the church would be truly hungry and thirsty for the things of God. If we would only be open to receive what He has for us, there would be no stopping the Kingdom. Many things are about to happen and I am preparing for what is to come. God is so good and worthy.

I have learned much through many conflicts, opinion, and judgments. Even though we are different and use different methods, we are all one family, God's family.   Just because you are in a different stream (church) doesn't make you different. After everything is said and done, all streams lead to a river. There, all the water mixes and becomes one flow. It is God's River. One flow, one family.

I have learned to be patient and to walk in love and peace. He has put me in the fire and I have come out. I will most certainly be refined again and again. I have been hurt, slandered and lied about. But so was my Lord. I have learned to submit but not lay down. He has made me as a watchman on the wall and until He says go, I will not give up my post.

Yes, I sometimes am fearful for much has been bestowed upon me and with it much responsibility. I go on praying that God's hand will direct me and He will keep me from using what He has given wrongly and out of His will. I weep when I think of the days, weeks, months and years that I let pass by, and the opportunities I missed by not using a gift for fear of man and their opinions. No more. With God's help, no man or woman will blind me again. My eyes are focused on the One I must follow and with His grace I will stir the gifts that are within me. Many have been brought to my side that have rekindled what once flowed in me so easily. My faith is increasing by His power and I am, once again, being used by Him and Him alone.

With all this said, (there is so much more that could be said). Let your eyes not be cast on any man, for no man can fill your soul. Always must you test the words of others and only listen to God. May grace, peace and joy always abound in your souls until the day of His arrival when we will finally behold our King, Master, Brother, Friend, the Lover of our souls. May the words of this testimony give you encouragement and fill you with the hope of your calling. For we all are called to a perfect walk in Him and for Him. Walk the walk and fight the fight that is put before you. With God by your side and within you there is no foe that can win. For greater is He that is within you than he who is in the world. We are kings and priests of the Most High God, and it is time we started to behave like it. Be blessed with the blessings of the King who is above all kings.

I need You Lord

More than the air that enters my lungs
I need You like the earth needs the sun,
like the birds need the sky.
I need You more than the food that sustains my body.
Lord I need You more than life itself.
As years go by and I wonder at the works of Your hands,
I can't imagine being without You
I can't fathom an existence void of Your presence
and Your love . I love You Lord.
Being in Your presence is more than words can express.
To be in Your Glory, in Your mere essence,
is beyond feeling. Beyond breath.
I need You, I want all I can get of You.

I wish to be possessed by Your Spirit and Your power.
To know nothing but You... in the silence of Your energy.
It is bliss. All consuming, all engulfing.
None can compare.
To be with You is all I want or need.
I want to run thru the fields of grass once more.
I want to lay my head upon Your lap as You caress me.
I want to just look into your eyes,
and get lost in the vastness of Your love for me.
Father, King, Lover of my soul, the very thing
that keeps the universe from falling apart is within me.
You are within me. How awesome is Your very existence.
Your very aroma is intoxicating
All I want is more and more of You.

Made in the USA
Middletown, DE
14 March 2016